Marx and Engels' *Communist Manifesto*

ALSO AVAILABLE FROM BLOOMSBURY

Aristotle's 'Politics': A Reader's Guide, Judith A. Swanson
Badiou's 'Being and Event': A Reader's Guide, Christopher Norris
Berkeley's 'Principles of Human Knowledge': A Reader's Guide, Alasdair Richmond
Deleuze and Guattari's 'What is Philosophy?': A Reader's Guide, Rex Butler
Deleuze's 'Difference and Repetition': A Reader's Guide, Joe Hughes
Descartes' 'Meditations': A Reader's Guide, Richard Francks
Hegel's 'Phenomenology of Spirit': A Reader's Guide, Stephen Houlgate
Heidegger's 'Being and Time': A Reader's Guide, William Blattner
Hobbes's 'Leviathan': A Reader's Guide, Laurie M. Johnson Bagby
Kant's 'Critique of Aesthetic Judgement': A Reader's Guide, Fiona Hughes
Kierkegaard's 'Fear and Trembling': A Reader's Guide, Clare Carlisle
Locke's 'Second Treatise of Government': A Reader's Guide, Paul Kelly
Nietzsche's 'Beyond Good and Evil': A Reader's Guide, Christa Davis Acampora and Keith Ansell Pearson
Nietzsche's 'Thus Spoke Zarathustra': A Reader's Guide, Clancy Martin
Rousseau's 'The Social Contract': A Reader's Guide, Christopher Wraight
Spinoza's 'Ethics': A Reader's Guide, J. Thomas Cook
Wittgenstein's 'Philosophical Investigations': A Reader's Guide, Arif Ahmed

Forthcoming from Bloomsbury

Kant's 'Critique of Practical Reason': A Reader's Guide, Courtney D. Fugate
Kant's 'Religion within the Boundaries of Mere Reason': A Reader's Guide, Eddis N. Miller
Levinas's 'Totality and Infinity': A Reader's Guide, William Large

A READER'S GUIDE

Marx and Engels' *Communist Manifesto*

PETER LAMB

Bloomsbury Academic
An imprint of Bloomsbury Publishing Plc

BLOOMSBURY
LONDON • NEW DELHI • NEW YORK • SYDNEY

Bloomsbury Academic
An imprint of Bloomsbury Publishing Plc

50 Bedford Square	1385 Broadway
London	New York
WC1B 3DP	NY 10018
UK	USA

www.bloomsbury.com

BLOOMSBURY and the Diana logo are trademarks of Bloomsbury Publishing Plc

First published 2015
Reprinted by Bloomsbury Academic 2015

© Peter Lamb, 2015

Peter Lamb has asserted his right under the Copyright, Designs and Patents Act, 1988, to be identified as the Author of this work.

All rights reserved. No part of this publication may be reproduced or transmitted in any form or by any means, electronic or mechanical, including photocopying, recording, or any information storage or retrieval system, without prior permission in writing from the publishers.

No responsibility for loss caused to any individual or organization acting on or refraining from action as a result of the material in this publication can be accepted by Bloomsbury or the author.

British Library Cataloguing-in-Publication Data
A catalogue record for this book is available from the British Library.

ISBN: PB: 978-1-47251-236-9
HB: 978-1-47250-678-8
ePDF: 978-1-47250-809-6
ePub: 978-1-47250-748-8

Library of Congress Cataloging-in-Publication Data
Lamb, Peter, 1960–
Marx and Engels' 'Communist manifesto': a reader's guide / Peter Lamb.
pages cm. – (Reader's guides)
Includes bibliographical references.
ISBN 978-1-4725-1236-9 (pbk.) – ISBN 978-1-4725-0678-8 (hardback)
1. Marx, Karl, 1818-1883. Manifest der Kommunistischen Partei.
2. Communism. 3. Socialism. I. Title.
HX39.5.A523L36 2015
335.4'22–dc23
2014032668

Typeset by Newgen Knowledge Works (P) Ltd., Chennai, India
Printed and bound in Great Britain

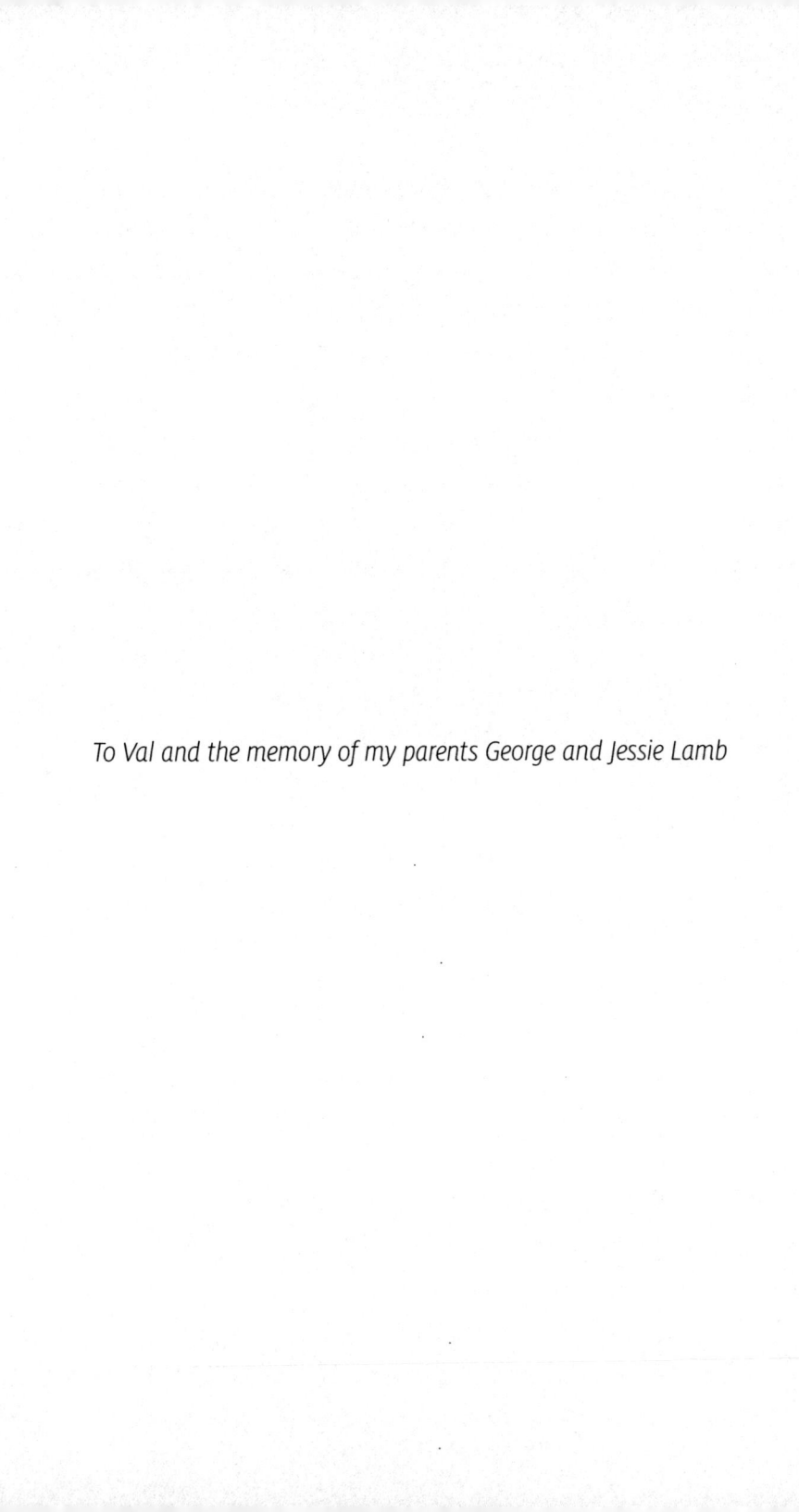

To Val and the memory of my parents George and Jessie Lamb

CONTENTS

Acknowledgements viii
A note on sources ix

Introduction 1
1 Context 3
2 Overview of themes 13
3 Reading the text 23
4 Reception and influence 133
5 Further reading 147

Notes 159
Index 171

ACKNOWLEDGEMENTS

Sita Bali and the Institute of Applied Creative Thinking (I-ACT) at Staffordshire University helped me secure some valuable time to finish this book. Pauline Elkes encouraged me to do so. Terrell Carver kindly mentioned some points at which Marx has been translated incorrectly in the Moore version of the *Communist Manifesto*. Val Lamb provided valuable support, encouragement and intelligent discussion. I alone am responsible for any shortcomings of the book.

A NOTE ON SOURCES

In this guide I have, wherever possible, referenced sources that readers will find accessible. Page references in brackets in the text are to Karl Marx and Friedrich Engels, *The Communist Manifesto*. New Haven and London: Yale University Press, 2012. Many references to the works of Marx and Engels other than the *Manifesto* are to David McLellan's popular *Selected Writings* volume. For works or parts of works by Marx and Engels that are not included in that volume I have selected other reasonably inexpensive and/or accessible printed sources. There are also references to various introductory essays and excerpts from books and articles that are included in some of the recent editions of the *Communist Manifesto*. Readers will hopefully want to seek out the sources of the excerpts.

Introduction

In late 1847, Friedrich Engels finished his final draft of a political pamphlet which he subsequently passed on to his political and intellectual colleague Karl Marx for revision. Marx began the task of transforming and enlivening the piece. In February the following year, the document thereby produced jointly by these two revolutionary authors, aged 28 and 30 respectively, was published as the *Manifesto of the Communist Party*. During the nineteenth century, many editions of the *Manifesto* appeared in several languages, including Samuel Moore's English translation, which Engels authorized, read, and indeed approved before it was published in 1888 – five years after the death of Marx. This radical tract, its title often shortened to the *Communist Manifesto* or sometimes simply the *Manifesto*, has since been hugely influential, inspiring people and movements around the world to campaign for social change and for various conceptions of progress.

Marx's name thus became widely known. Indeed, of all the illustrious writers in the history of political thought, he is probably the most famous or, in the view of his opponents, infamous. In most editions of the *Manifesto*, Engels is justifiably named as the co-author. Hence, many readers begin to associate his work with that of Marx. Even if they have never read any of their works, many people with an interest in politics, history or philosophy are aware of their reputation for being great revolutionary writers. While for some this is a reputation to be admired, for others it is one to be condemned.

Many of those who do come to appreciate the historical and theoretical importance of the pamphlet begin to take a very different view of the world than they had previously held. A large number of those people have, since 1848, gone on to consider themselves Marxists in one or more of three ways: in personal conviction, as intellectuals or as political activists.[1] Even if they do not associate themselves in any of these ways with the views of Marx and Engels, many readers nevertheless find that the *Manifesto* holds their interest immediately. This is not least because of its very lively, dynamic and forceful style.

Notwithstanding the initial attraction of the *Manifesto*, it is not unusual for those who delve further into the text to find some of the jargon in the pamphlet rather obscure. Much of the detail can, moreover, initially be difficult to grasp. This reader's guide intends, therefore, to help foster a better understanding and appreciation of the *Manifesto*. Chapter one discusses the intellectual and political environment of the pamphlet's appearance in the mid-nineteenth century. This includes a brief look at the converging career paths of the two authors who produced it for the newly formed, small, but highly motivated Communist League and saw it through to publication in the year of uprisings in Europe. In Chapter two, the main themes are outlined before the far longer Chapter three examines the work in more detail. Subsequently, Chapter four offers a concise discussion of the pamphlet's reception and influence. Many readers reach the end of the *Manifesto* and seek thereafter to find out more about Marx, Engels and the tradition they started. The final chapter of this guide, therefore, offers advice on further reading.

In preparation for study of the *Manifesto*, some awareness of its historical context is invaluable. Any discussion of the pamphlet must, indeed, locate its publication in the particular circumstances of 1848. This was a year characterized by attempts to begin the revolution in many parts of Europe. It is to that context that we now turn.

CHAPTER ONE

Context

The radical activity of 1848 constituted an important episode in the development of the international labour movement, within which the Communist League was a revolutionary player. In order to gain a fuller understanding of this development, the events of 1848 must be seen in their broader historical, economic, social and political setting. A wave of uprisings against the established social and political orders swept Europe that year. This was the climax to a period that, having begun with the outbreak of the French Revolution in 1789, is sometimes known as the 'epoch of the dual revolution'.[1] The reason for labelling this epoch, or period, as such is that it was characterized not only by the political revolution that had erupted in France, but also by the industrial revolution. Starting in Great Britain, the process of this 'revolution' accelerated in the early nineteenth century with the development of the railways and spread to Western Europe and the United States. The combination of political and industrial revolutions had enhanced the political and economic power of a social class that held significant shares of capital (or in other words of the property and equipment needed to conduct industrial and financial business). This class came to be known as the bourgeoisie. Even in those European countries where formal political power remained in the hands of monarchies, the influence of the bourgeoisie on the decision-making processes was growing. This gain was not shared with others in society, even though the French Revolution had promised liberty and equality for humanity. The working classes and peasantry indeed benefited very little from such progress in practice. Dissatisfaction and revolutionary attitudes thus began to stir in Europe, leading to the insurrections of 1848.

The publication of the *Manifesto*

Since the outbreak of the French Revolution, various groups whose members considered themselves to be communists or socialists had sought to harness the dissatisfaction. On this basis they began to perceive possibilities for social and political change. Marx and Engels grasped and built on the radicalism which had thus begun to brew.[2] When, in this environment in February 1848, the *Manifesto* was finished and sent for publication as a pamphlet for the Communist League, its drafter and final author were unwittingly laying the foundations of the movement that came to be known as Marxism. At the request of their comrades in the League, of which they had by then become prominent and influential members, they published the *Manifesto* in London. It began to appear in Paris later in February, less than a fortnight before the uprisings began in the latter city.

The insurrectionary activity quickly spread beyond the French capital to many other major European cities.[3] Rather than being either a stimulus or a response to the unsuccessful revolutionary efforts of 1848, the *Manifesto* can, however, be seen as a tactical document intended to be a contribution to the broader cause and campaign.[4] Indeed, as the pamphlet had only begun to appear in print for the first time at the end of February, any influence upon the uprising in Paris that month can only have been upon an already-precipitated campaign. While the Communist League did play a significant role in the attempted German Revolution of May, the *Manifesto* would have been received in April by activists there whose work had already begun.[5]

It would be wrong, furthermore, to assume that the uprisings of 1848 were the practical reflection of a firmly established and unanimously embraced doctrine of communism in the broader workers' movement. Before Marx and Engels had employed the term 'communist' for their famous work, early notions of communism, while varying considerably, were generally republican and egalitarian. These were characteristics that were not generally associated with socialism at the time. Although the terms 'communist' and 'socialist' had sometimes been used interchangeably, socialism was often considered to be more concerned with association and cooperation than with republicanism and egalitarianism. Nevertheless, all socialists and communists considered some kind of social and political change for the benefit of ordinary people to be possible and desirable.

In their contribution to this broader movement, inspired by their growing confidence in the prospects for change, Marx and Engels drew in the *Manifesto* upon some tenets that had been associated with earlier versions of communism and some that had been linked with socialism. They nevertheless also offered, with recourse to some brief examples, bitter criticism of many of the ways in which the tenets had thus been previously employed. Furthermore, and crucially, they presented their critical analysis of capitalism, at the heart of which were their distinctive conceptions of class relations and class struggle.[6] The belief they presented in the possibility of radical and fundamental change as a result of the struggle reflected the industrial and scientific developments of their times. Such developments, while bringing misery to the many and great wealth to the few in those times, could, if suitably harnessed, be utilized in order to provide the conditions for and means to a better life for humanity. As will hopefully become clear in the course of this guide, the combination of critical analysis of these developments and consideration of their potential was a key thread of the pamphlet.

The efforts of Marx and Engels did not, however, have their intended impact in the short term. The revolutions of 1848 soon fizzled out and the *Manifesto* would enjoy only a very narrow readership until it was revived in the early 1870s.[7] As will be discussed in Chapter four of this guide, the influence of the *Manifesto* grew thereafter. Sometimes this growth was gradual and at other times more rapid in political environments that changed considerably in terms of both time and location.

That the *Manifesto* did eventually become hugely influential reflects not least the abrasive, strident and thereby exciting nature of its argument and rhetoric. Marx and Engels thereby made a distinctive and innovative theoretical contribution to the broader radical tradition – a tradition that, as we have just seen, had shot to prominence in the several years of upheaval that followed the outbreak of the French Revolution of 1789. The powerful prose that Marx used to convey his message in the pamphlet upon receiving the draft from Engels will be discussed in Chapter three. At this point, however, in order to appreciate why the pamphlet was conceived in the first place, it will be useful to focus briefly on the intellectual development of these two collaborators in the years prior to 1848 and during the production of this famous text.

The authors

Born in 1820 to a wealthy businessman, Engels was brought up in the German Rhineland town of Barmen. His hometown is difficult to find on maps today, as in 1929 (34 years after his death) Barmen would merge with Elberfeld and several other towns to form the city of Wuppertal. Working for his father's company as a young man, Engels gained direct experience of capitalism. This job did not, however, satisfy his intellectual and recreational appetite. Hence, he danced, rode horses, swam and participated in debating clubs – the latter being an activity which combined intense philosophical conversation with heavy drinking. He also produced radical journalistic articles that were published in some of the more progressive newspapers of the region. Disenchanted with the protestant beliefs on which he had been brought up, he came to reject religion itself. He also embraced radical interpretations of the ideas of G. W. F. Hegel, especially those concerning the dialectic.[8]

The Hegelian dialectic has acquired a reputation for being quite daunting. This, however, is not really warranted, as its core point is quite simple. In summary, it holds that spirit, or mind has developed throughout history, gradually improving societies and enhancing the freedom of people who composed them. Hegel implied that, with its liberal reforms that had been introduced after Napoleon Bonaparte's victory over its former rulers, the state in Prussia was at the most advanced stage of freedom yet to be attained. Nevertheless, the liberal reforms were soon replaced by new reactionary policies and the Prussian state became increasingly conservative. Some enthusiasts for Hegel's political philosophy continued to suggest that despite this conservative drift Prussia was his ideal state. Radicals among the Young Hegelian intellectual movement disagreed, however, stressing that he considered the present society to be no more than one of the phases in the dialectical process.

Ludwig Feuerbach, who was one of the radical Young Hegelians, argued furthermore that existence actually precedes thought, rather than the other way around. Engels, significantly, approved of Feuerbach's position. Although this was in effect to step outside Hegelianism rather than to extend it, the belief in a dialectical process of history had become securely lodged in Engels' worldview. It will be useful to bear this belief in mind when, in Chapter three, we come to grips with the argument that he helped Marx construct for publication in the *Manifesto*.

It was not philosophy alone which cultivated in Engels' mind the ideas that would inspire him to work with Marx on the *Manifesto*. When he moved to England in the early 1840s to work for his father's business in Manchester, he witnessed at first hand the abject poverty and desperate living and working conditions of the working class (indeed, he was guided through even the most dangerous parts of Manchester by his working-class lover Mary Burns). He began to perceive these conditions as direct consequences of the capitalist system. The industrial working class that sold its labour for a wage – a class which he and Marx consistently referred to as the proletariat – had not only been created artificially by that system, but would also be at the forefront of the movement to replace it with a better society. Engels had thus begun to conceive of historical development.[9] He published the result of his study of working-class life, titled *The Condition of the Working Class in England*, in German in 1845 (but not in English until 1885).[10] He was thus ready to combine his philosophy with political economy in two important drafts of the *Manifesto* with which Marx would subsequently work. As will be discussed at a number of places in Chapter three of the present guide, those drafts, which would later be published with the titles 'Draft of a Communist Confession of Faith' and 'Principles of Communism', are of considerable value to the understanding of some of the important points that Marx would go on to make in the pamphlet.

Marx's intellectual development had led him into collaboration with Engels several years before they worked together on the *Manifesto*. Born in the Rhineland, Marx experienced a rather different upbringing and education from that which Engels experienced in the region. Marx's rearing was indeed a liberal and humanist one in his home city of Trier. His father Heschel had been born into an influential Jewish family but converted to Protestantism when the Rhineland, having been occupied by Napoleon, passed into Prussian hands. Prussia increased restrictions on the career paths open to Jews. Therefore, Heschel, who as a humanist was of course not enthusiastically religious, converted in order to allow him to continue with his work as a lawyer. He subsequently changed his name from the Jewish Heschel to Hienrich. As an aficionado of the rationalist and liberal ideas of the Enlightenment, Hienrich sent Karl to a school with a humanist ethos. Karl's work shows that he took to Enlightenment ideas very well.[11]

To continue his education Karl went to the university in Bonn; but his father withdrew him after only one year. Marx senior had disapproved for a wide variety of reasons, including his son's enrolment in too many courses, his heavy drinking and fighting and eventually his tendency to be more interested in poetry than in law. So Karl Marx transferred to Berlin University in October 1936, having become formally engaged with Jenny von Westphalen during the summer [12] Jenny and Karl went on to have six children – three of whom died tragically in infancy.[13]

As a student in Berlin, Marx developed an interest in the philosophy of Hegel, of which he became increasingly critical. Like Engels, he became involved with the Young Hegelians. Marx decided to pursue an academic career and so he remained at the University of Berlin to write his doctoral thesis. Tactically, judging that his argument would be received more sympathetically at the University of Jena, he submitted his thesis at the latter institution instead. He graduated in 1841.

The hostility in authoritarian Prussia to radical philosophy rendered Marx's chances of gaining a secure academic post very slim. Subsequently, he decided to pursue a career in journalism. However, his work as an editor and writer for the *Rheinische Zeitung* newspaper was suppressed and he decided to leave Prussia in order to be able to express his views more freely. Shortly before he embarked on the journey to make his new home in Paris, he had drafted an article which was significant for its insistence that economics, rather than politics or religion, was the source of the most fundamental problem of modern society. The article, titled 'On the Jewish Question', was a critique of the work of Bruno Bauer who not only disapproved of the Christian state for its restrictions on the rights of Jews, but also criticized Jews themselves for expecting the enjoyment of civil rights without renouncing their own religion. Marx argued that the problem was neither the Jewish faith nor the Christian state in particular but, rather, the modern state itself. While the state focused on political rights, individualism flourished in civil society, meaning that social rights were ignored. The predominantly egoistic character of human beings cultivated in capitalist society was thus made to seem natural. This disguised the fact that economic life, rather than religious or philosophical doctrine, was at the root of human alienation. Alienation prevented people from enjoying their lives as community-oriented species beings. The use of money, which had in fact brought this situation about, was the greatest barrier to human freedom.[14] He presented this notion of alienation in greater detail in a work that, unpublished until 1932, is now known as the 'Economic and Philosophical Manuscripts'.[15]

'On the Jewish Question' was one of two articles that Marx published in 1844 in a short-lived German-language newspaper, *Deutsch-Französische Jahbücher*, which was based in Paris. The other was 'Towards a Critique of Hegel's Philosophy of Right: Introduction', which, like 'On the Jewish Question', voiced ideas that would be built on to produce some of the prominent features of the *Manifesto*, such as the portrayal of the proletariat as the class with radical chains. Humanity would be emancipated if those chains were broken. This would happen because the proletariat could emancipate other spheres of society by liberating itself. Emancipation of the German proletariat could develop into, and indeed would require for its maintenance, broader human emancipation. This point was not developed into a clear account of the way this might happen but, essentially, he meant that this was the case because to bring an end to the universal suffering of the proletariat would require human redemption in general.[16]

Deutsch-Französische Jahbücher was suppressed in Prussia after the first double issue and did not have sufficient readers in France to make it a viable publication. By March 1844, it had therefore ceased production. Nevertheless, many of the ideas Marx had expressed in it would remain to the fore of his thought. Not least in this respect was the view that in Germany, which was at that time one of the parts of Europe in which capitalism was relatively undeveloped, the proletariat could be emancipated as part of a broader, international revolution. This would become an important point in the final section of the *Communist Manifesto*.

Marx and Engels as collaborators

The collaboration of the two revolutionary authors began in August 1844, when Marx received a visit in Paris from Engels. When they had first met briefly in 1842 as journalists with growing reputations, these two future comrades were wary of each other as rivals.[17] This time, however, they entered into a professional and personal friendship which they would maintain until the death of Marx 33 years later. Indeed, as a result of this early meeting, they engaged in intense discussion for ten days leading to the writing of two of their most significant jointly authored works: *The Holy Family* and *The German Ideology*. In these two works they developed the materialist conception of history, which would underpin the ideas that were later presented in the *Manifesto*.

The metaphorical 'family' in the rather strangely titled *The Holy Family* consisted of Bauer and his intellectual circle, who were criticized by Marx and Engels for continuing to argue that spirit is the progressive force in history. Marx and Engels stressed that it was the movement of the masses that constituted the progressive force. This movement would take shape when the people who comprised the proletariat were able to overcome the alienation and dehumanization that resulted from the system of private property. In this work they portrayed socialism and communism as presenting a materialist doctrine.[18] As will be discussed later in this guide, Marx had by 1848 come to take a more unfavourable view of many doctrines he included in the socialist category, approving by way of contrast the more radical communist approach.

Just before *The Holy Family* went to press, Marx's journalistic work attracted the wrong sort of attention. He had in the summer of 1844 accepted the opportunity to write in the German-language communist paper *Vorwärts!*, which was the only uncensored radical journal published in that language. The content of the paper came, however, to the attention of the Prussian government, which subsequently complained to the French king who demanded the closure of the paper in January 1845. Marx, moreover, was expelled from France and so he went to live in the Belgian capital

Brussels.[19] In an important step in their growing intellectual bonding process, Engels decided to go to Belgium for a period of work with Marx.[20]

A substantial project on which Marx and Engels embarked during this period was their intensive study of German philosophy. The result of their endeavours was the substantial, two-volume work *The German Ideology*, which they wrote over a period spanning 1845 and 1846. In this study, Marx and Engels argued for the abolition of private property. This would, in turn, they believed, bring an end to alienation. The materialist conception of history took shape in the course of this work as they reasoned that the socioeconomic process represented the basis of human society. Politics, law and religion were therefore all built upon this base. The division of labour, they suggested, developed as big business came to dominate the economy. As this division grew, the productive forces seemed to be independent of individuals.

The term 'productive forces' is crucial in the ideas of Marx and Engels. As has been summarised concisely by Gill Hands in her introductory book on Marx, they used the term to signify the 'combination of the means of production, e.g. factories and machinery, with labour power'.[21] Because the division of labour served to propagate the impression that productive forces were independent of one another, what was obscured was the fact that such forces could only operate through the interaction and association of the individuals of which society was composed. This fact went largely unnoticed and so the fundamental social change that was necessary for the further development of the productive forces was thwarted. Marx and Engels stressed the need for the revolutionary replacement of the present form of society with an arrangement based on communism. Productive forces would thus be brought under the control of the workers.

The German Ideology was not published until 1932, long after the deaths of its authors. Marx joked in 1859 that he and Engels had abandoned the manuscript 'to the gnawing criticism of the mice' after a publisher had pulled out of an arrangement to print it.[22] They had decided anyway, Marx added, that they had by then achieved their main intention of self-clarification. The importance of the book for readers of the present guide, however, lies in the progress it reveals in the development of key themes that would feature in the *Manifesto*. The notion of productive forces, the materialist conception of history and the ideas for a new society to replace capitalism were all being thought through as Marx and Engels worked on *The German Ideology*.

Even before *The German Ideology* was finished, Marx had taken steps to form a Communist Correspondence Committee. The aim was to coordinate communism in theory and practice between activists in the capital cities of Europe. The Committee created crucial ties between Marx and Engels on the one hand and the communists of London on the other. These ties helped create the network that transformed an organization known as the League of the Just into the Communist League.[23]

When in 1847 the League commissioned Marx to write the *Manifesto*, Engels did the groundwork in the form of two drafts (which, as mentioned earlier, were titled 'Draft of a Communist Confession of Faith' and 'Principles of Communism'), which proved to be crucial to the main argument of the pamphlet. Engels wrote each of these pieces in the form of questions and answers about communism and why it was required. This form of writing is known as a catechism, and the drafts with which we are concerned are usually described as such. The style in which these drafts on the one hand and the *Manifesto* on the other were written was thus very different, the latter being far livelier. Nevertheless, the similarities in content between 'Principles of Communism' and the final published work show that Engels played a very major role along with Marx, certainly deserving recognition as co-author.[24]

Together, Marx and Engels thereby produced one of the most influential political pamphlets in the history of political thought. The details of the work will be examined carefully in what is by far the largest chapter of the present guide. Before that, however, the next chapter prepares the stage by outlining the key themes of the *Manifesto*.

CHAPTER TWO

Overview of themes

The *Manifesto's* prominent key themes included the epoch of the bourgeoisie, class struggle and proletarian revolution, variants of socialism and the measures that the communists would seek to achieve after the revolution. These themes are discussed later in this chapter. First, though, it is useful to focus briefly on a broader theme within which Marx and Engels shaped their main argument. Many years later in 1880, in both his major work *Socialism: Utopian and Scientific* and a letter to the socialist editor of the journal *Der sozialistiche Akademiker*, Engels would refer to this broader theme — mentioned several times already in the previous chapter of this guide — as the materialist conception of history.[1]

The materialist conception of history

The material conception of history, as formulated by Engels, signified that any social structure is based on two interdependent processes. The first and most fundamental of these processes is the production of things necessary for life. The social structure is based, secondly, upon the exchange of those products. Throughout history, the manner in which society was divided into classes varied in line with changes to the ways in which such processes took place. Social change and revolution brought about transformations of those ways. Although human thought was obviously one major driving force behind such developments, a fundamental factor underpinning them was that of revolutionary changes in the modes of production. The proletarian revolution would lead to the next such change.[2]

Engels' materialist conception of history has often been employed in the literature on Marx and Marxists to summarise their key views. Many people are, hence, surprised to find that neither this term nor 'historical materialism', as the conception is sometimes called, was ever actually used in the *Manifesto* or indeed in any other piece that Marx wrote. The ideas it represented did, however, constitute a central, implicit theme in the pamphlet as well as in a number of his other works. This is particularly evident in a short piece that has come to be one of Marx's most well-known and widely read writings, 'Preface to *A Critique of Political Economy*', which he wrote and published in 1859. For this reason, it is useful in the present guide to keep hold of the notion of a 'materialist conception of history' for the purpose of offering a brief outline of the set of ideas to which it refers. One should be careful, however, not to attribute the notion to Marx.

Turning to the work of 1859, although few people today read *A Critique of Political Economy* in its entirety, very many more who take an interest in Marx soon become familiar with a brief outline of what he called his guiding thread, which he presented in its Preface. Bearing in mind the key points of Engels' materialist conception of history, it is in fact very useful to consider the guiding thread in such terms as one begins to study the *Manifesto* for the first time. The Preface is, moreover, essential reading for anybody who has tackled the *Manifesto* and wants to gain a fuller understanding of Marx's thought in general.

Society, Marx suggested in the guiding thread outlined in the 1859 Preface, goes through different stages in history as productive forces become increasingly advanced. During each stage there are relations of production between dominant and dominated classes. These relations can be considered together to form the economic structure of the society. The nature of the relations of production will largely depend on the productive forces. So, for example, when those forces are suitably advanced they allow capitalism to take the place of feudalism. The productive forces and relations of production of any period in time in a society together constitute the mode of production.

The relations of power in the political, legal, educational and other institutions, which can together be seen to comprise the infrastructure of society, reflect the mode of production. The dominant class can thus rule because its ideas prevail in society. Each stage ends, however, when the productive forces, such as human capability and technology, are so developed that the existing type of society becomes outdated. The dominant ideas are challenged and a new stage begins. In the industrial capitalist society, the capitalist class (bourgeoisie) was dominant and the class of wage-labourers (proletariat) was dominated. Marx said this stage would end in liberation by means of revolution, as the proletariat would challenge the dominant ideas and structure of the capitalist society. The result of the successful challenge would be the introduction of a new society in which the antagonistic form of previous modes of production would have no place. He identified the *Manifesto* as one of the key works that contributed to the formulation of this guiding thread of his work.[3]

As we saw in the previous chapter, Marx and Engels had been developing the elements of this broader theme in some of their earlier writings. Significantly, as Jonathan Wolff has made very clear, this materialist conception of history should not be confused with basic materialism or Idealism. The first of these two alternatives neglects the role that humans play in creating and changing the world in which they live, while the second interprets historical development in terms of the development of thought. The materialist conception of history helps one recognize that in order to understand society it is important to pay attention to, first, the material conditions of the natural world; second, the historical development of such conditions; and third, to the role that people play in physically bringing about such development.[4]

Readers will, perhaps, find it useful at this point to focus on and digest the key points of Engels' materialist conception of history that have been introduced in this section. Without, first, having a grasp of this conception, and, second, noting how it serves to summarise a crucial element in the thought of Marx and Engels, one can quite easily misinterpret some of the key points in the *Manifesto*. It would, then, be a good idea to stop and reflect on the conception as a guiding thread before turning to the first of the particular key themes – that of the epoch of the bourgeoisie.

The epoch of the bourgeoisie

As mentioned earlier, Marx used the term 'bourgeoisie' to refer to a social class that held significant shares of the property and equipment that were needed to conduct industrial and financial business. These holdings are known as capital. The *Manifesto* includes some instances where Marx used the term 'capitalists' to portray this class; but far more often in that pamphlet he used the term 'bourgeoisie' for this purpose. Engels and he were concerned with, first, the role of this bourgeois class in the political, social and economic structure of their times; second, the way in which this class had achieved such a prominent role; and third, the means by which that role would end.

The epoch of the bourgeoisie (an epoch being a period in time having distinctive features) was the term Marx used in the first main section of the *Manifesto* to describe the capitalist era that people were experiencing in the nineteenth century. Although Marx was condemning this period as one of exploitation, he was also in fact stressing the positive function that the epoch was having in the development of conditions suitable for the new socialist and eventually communist society that revolution would bring about. As Peter Osborne has emphasized in his introductory guide, Marx and Engels were thus thinkers of what would later become known as 'modernity'.[5]

Modernity is a perceived condition based on an experience and depiction of society in a particular era. As such, modernity illustrates what is new in society and what is likely to result from these new features in the future. Marx had, indeed, expressed this sense of modernity in *The Poverty of Philosophy* the year before the *Manifesto* was published. As productive forces developed, modes of production were subject to change. This in turn led to a transformation of social relations. As he put it: 'The hand-mill gives you society with the feudal lord; the steam-mill, society with the industrial capitalist.'[6] Although this change had transferred power from one dominant class to an even more exploitative one (the capitalists or bourgeoisie), the development constituted progress. This was because the steam mill could be employed in a future society to produce goods for all to enjoy. For such a situation to transpire, however, there would need to be a class struggle. This brings our discussion to another key theme of the *Manifesto*.

Class struggle and the proletarian revolution

In the *Manifesto*, Marx and Engels said that the history of society was actually characterized by class struggles. To prepare the way for the detailed analysis of the pamphlet in the next chapter of this guide, it is important to note here just what, broadly, they meant by class. It is also useful at this point to establish briefly just what the proletarian class struggle was in fact all about.

Readers will not find a clear and concise definition of class in the works of Marx and Engels. While this does make the understanding of the key points of the *Manifesto* slightly more difficult to achieve than if one were available, it is perhaps worthwhile to bear in mind that it is actually not unusual for thinkers to refrain from spelling out the meaning of each of the main terms they use in their works. Marx and Engels are probably among many who have not done so because they simply felt no need to state the terms of debates that had been played out for some time and in which they were now participating. In Marx's case, in a letter of 1852 to fellow Communist League member Joseph Weydemeyer, one finds him insisting upon receiving no credit for the discovery of classes, the struggle between them or their anatomy.[7]

In the absence of a clear and concise definition, it is, however, possible to detect in the work of Marx and Engels a broad interpretation of class. A class is perceived in their writings as a type of people, members of which have previously organized or will at some point organize on the basis of their needs and actively seek to transform society.[8] The bourgeoisie as a class had achieved such transformation and the proletariat would be the next class to do so. In a piece which he wrote and published in 1850 titled '1848–49' (republished by Engels in 1895 under the title *The Class Struggles in France*), Marx discussed the situation in which the composition of the bourgeois class in France differed from its counterpart in England. The industrial faction of the bourgeoisie in France, unlike in England, failed to enjoy dominance within the broader bourgeois class. Hence, in the revolutionary events of February 1848, this industrial faction had not initially considered that its interests coincided with those of the broader class. Those events had sharpened the wits of this industrial faction which, realizing that it was threatened by a workers' revolution, became the most fanatical collective member of the party of order which represented the broader bourgeoisie.[9] This interpretation is consistent with an understanding of class in terms of transformation and organization on the basis of need. The bourgeoisie had transformed society according to its needs, and the industrial faction within it realized that to organize on such a basis of need meant organizing within the broader class. This understanding can be recognized in the letter to Weydemeyer, where Marx stressed that one of the things that his own work did prove was that the existence of classes was 'bound up with particular phases in the development of production'.[10] This, moreover, helps bear out the interpretation discussed earlier of Marx as a thinker of modernity.

The conditions of modernity were developing the capitalist structure to the degree to which there could actually be abundance for all. Before such abundance could thus be enjoyed universally, however, the exploitation of the working class, or proletariat, by the bourgeoisie would need to be abolished. Furthermore, bourgeois exploitation of the world market – a process that was implanting the bourgeois mode of production throughout the world – would need to be terminated. As will be discussed later, Marx believed it would only be a matter of time before the methods and practices of the bourgeoisie would lead the entire mode of production to come crashing down, with the helpful hand of the proletariat. This, however, would require effective political organization. In the *Manifesto*, Marx dismissed the ideas held by a range of socialist thinkers whose proposals for organization he criticized as inadequate to the task. He considered proletarian revolution, in which the workers would themselves play a key role rather than simply accept doctrines created for them, to be crucial to the success of the struggle.

Variants of socialism and communism

Marx contrasted his own ideas with those of other socialists and communists throughout much of his adult life. This was partly due to the inflexibility of some his rivals and partly because others among them believed socialism could be built in new communities without a radical break from the extant economic system. In the latter case, Marx actually differed from Engels who took great interest in ideas concerning such communities. This divergence of views was resolved in Marx's favour when he decided to omit a proposal for the formation of socialist communities that Engels had made in the final draft of what would become the *Manifesto*.[11] Marx considered plans for such communities to be pointless, the main task instead being to organize politically in anticipation of the point at which the development of productive forces would reach the stage whereby they could produce abundance for all. The situation would thus become suitable for revolutionary action by the proletariat in order to overthrow the existing system in its entirety.

Marx made criticism of rival socialist and communist ideas a prominent theme in the *Manifesto* in which he tried to steer a course between two sorts of thought. On the one hand, there were people in whose ideas, as he saw it, class struggle did not feature strongly enough. In the pamphlet he classified many such thinkers among three categories which he devised for this purpose. On the other hand, he mentioned, albeit very briefly, that the conspiratorial strategies and austere goals of old-style communists were inadequate. Furthermore, he considered that those who believed that class struggle could be successful without any sort of alliance with some other segments of society misunderstood what was necessary in order to challenge the existing holders of power.[12] He would continue to insist on such alliances long after the first publication of the *Manifesto*. Indeed, he stressed in his 'Critique of the Gotha Programme' in 1875 that it was incorrect to consider all classes other than the proletariat as constituting a single reactionary mass. His socialist rival Ferdinand Lassalle was, he insisted moreover, wrong in suggesting that the *Manifesto* had considered all other classes as such.[13]

This stress on the need for collaboration serves as another indication that Marx and Engels were concerned with the progress that could be made before the eventual outbreak of proletarian revolution. As mentioned earlier, this was a concern with the possibilities of what would today be called modernity. This optimistic element of their thought allowed them to turn their attention to measures that should be taken after the revolution.

After the revolution

In the *Manifesto*, Marx listed the measures to be implemented once the revolution reached the stage where it would be able to remove the bourgeoisie from power. These measures included, among others, the abolition of property in land and centralization of credit in the hands of the state. This would be a temporary stage in order to prepare the way for a new communist society. Elsewhere in his writings Marx called this stage the 'dictatorship of the proletariat'[14] – a term that would cause much controversy in the twentieth century when V. I. Lenin, Josef Stalin and others, influenced by the work of Marx, introduced actual dictatorial regimes.

Perhaps, surprisingly, Marx did not go on in the *Manifesto* to discuss the features of the communist society in any detail. In fact, Engels and he said little about this future society in their other writings. In *The German Ideology* they did discuss this future society briefly. It would be based on communal property and served by highly developed productive forces. Private property would be abolished, as would the division of labour, and people would not be tied to particular occupations. There would no longer be a division between particular interests of individuals and the common interest of society. This would, however, require a new way of thinking and the development of human nature, which was indeed malleable. Therefore, traits such as greed and envy would disappear.[15] Almost 30 years later in 'Critique of the Gotha Programme' he distinguished between the lower and higher stages of communism. In the lower stage, workers would receive back the equivalent of what they would produce, except for deductions for society. In the higher stage, people would contribute to society according to their ability and receive according to their needs.[16] There is, however, no extensive plan to be found in this work.

Perhaps, if asked about this omission, Marx and Engels would have told their readers that of course they did not go into such detail about the higher stages of the communist society. Their worldview was not, after all, one of utopian socialism but, rather, one of concern with the problems of the existing society that were blocking the development of the productive forces. This concern needed to be expressed clearly and concisely because, without such development, communism would not be able to provide a better life for people in society. In the next chapter, this worldview as expressed in the *Manifesto* will be analysed in detail so that readers can gain the most from their study of this most famous political pamphlet.

CHAPTER THREE

Reading the text

This chapter is the largest and most important of the guide. The purpose of the previous chapters was, indeed, to pave way for this one. In the pages that follow, the *Manifesto* will be examined, analysed and discussed in some detail. This will help readers to understand more clearly its jargon, its difficult concepts and Marx's many references to people, a number of whom are relatively little-known today. These are features of the pamphlet which can make it a very difficult work to fully comprehend. Newcomers to Marx's work may, because of these features, be tempted to simply place the *Manifesto* back on the bookshelf. By reading this chapter, those newcomers will, hopefully, decide instead to persevere with their study of the pamphlet. By taking the latter course they may find that the ideas and purposes expressed by Marx, on the basis of Engels' drafts, may be grasped more firmly than an initial look at the *Manifesto* might lead one to believe.

Some of Marx's critics may argue that any attempt such as this to help clarify Marx's work and its intentions will almost immediately run up against an unassailable obstacle; this will happen, such critics sometimes suggest, because Marx was a rather muddled thinker whose various ideas do not fit together coherently. Jon Elster, for example, has suggested that a 'disturbing feature of Marx's historical theories and writings is their lack of integration with one another'. Marx, he went on, sometimes seems to have 'suffered from a severe lack of intellectual control'.[1] This guide presents a rather different picture. Careful analysis of various points in the *Manifesto*, sometimes supported by reference to selections from Marx and Engels' other writings, helps reveal that they did provide a coherent argument, even though Marx's stylistic and rhetorical exploits at times make this less than entirely clear.

In order to engage in this analytical task the sections of the *Manifesto* will, except for the prefaces which were added to the later editions, be discussed in this guide in the turn in which they appear in the published pamphlet. This will not only enable readers to use this guide more easily while following the text, but it will also help keep sight of the *Manifesto* as a piece of political writing prepared in a certain style and format for particular purposes. In order to help readers consolidate their understanding by focusing for a second time on some of the key points, each section will be followed by a few study questions related to the text and the issues and queries it raises.

The text to be followed and analysed is for the most part that of Moore's translation, which, as was mentioned earlier in this guide, gained the approval of Engels in 1888. There have been many editions, not least because of such approval, which have utilized this translation. The version of the Moore translation followed and referenced throughout this chapter is the one edited and presented by Jeffrey C. Isaac in 2012.[2] To help readers to use this guide without frequently turning to and from reference notes, page numbers of quotes and other passages from that edition are inserted in brackets at the appropriate places in the text. Nevertheless, occasional references will be made to other versions of the translation and, importantly, to Terrell Carver's more recent translation when this helps clarify Marx's points.

In contrast with some other versions of Moore's translation, Isaac places the usual selection of prefaces, two of which were written by Marx and Engels together and the others by Engels alone, after the main text. The simple reason for this ordering is that the prefaces were all written many years after the first edition. Hence, they refer in hindsight to some of the significant points that had been made in the original pamphlet and discuss further developments since that time. In utilizing Isaac's edition the present chapter likewise discusses the main text first. By turning to them after that text, readers are encouraged to consider the prefaces after having already analysed the key points. A clearer understanding will thereby be gained of what Marx and Engels, or in most cases Engels alone, had to say in those prefaces. This arrangement is especially useful to those beginning to read the *Manifesto* for the first time, as the prefaces contain some interesting passages that cannot really be appreciated unless one has gained at least a little awareness of the original material first.

It is fitting at this stage to reiterate and clarify another matter before commencing our examination of the text of the *Manifesto*. The main text was, as the previous chapters have indicated, the final version of the argument that Engels and Marx had developed together by the beginning of 1848. The *Manifesto* can, moreover, as has been discussed earlier in the guide, be considered as the culmination of several years of collaboration, and thus very much a joint effort of Marx and Engels. Although the words of the main text will be attributed to Marx as the author of the published version, the contribution of Engels as drafter and intellectual collaborator in the project is of course crucially important. This will become evident in the following pages, where the significance of some of the ideas offered by Engels in his drafts are recognized and discussed. Reference to those drafts will sometimes help clarify passages where Marx was, as mentioned earlier, less than entirely clear or, as is occasionally the case, where he was not at all clear.

It was, furthermore, Engels whose idea it was to present the pamphlet in a format other than the catechisms of which his drafts were comprised. He expressed this idea to Marx in a letter of 23/24 November 1847. In the same communication Engels recommended that the work be published with the title *Communist Manifesto*.[3]

One other acquaintance of Marx should, perhaps, also be mentioned briefly at this point in order to add a little more detail to our picture of the origins of the *Manifesto*. Marx, as will be seen later in this chapter, concluded with the now famous slogan: 'Working men of all countries unite!' (p. 102). This phrase was actually devised by the veteran revolutionary activist Karl Schapper during the reorganization of the League of the Just in the period of its transformation into the Communist League. Having been involved in radical politics since his student days in the early 1830s, Schapper had taken part in a series of failed insurrections which eventually led to his exile, his settlement in London and then his leading role in the League. Marx had leant on Schapper and the other prominent members of the League to find a replacement for the old slogan 'All Men are Brothers', which brushed over class division. Marx's adoption of his comrade's new slogan for use at the end of the *Manifesto* illustrates clearly that this was a pamphlet of a particular, campaigning political organization.[4]

The vibrant style which makes the *Manifesto* so readable is nevertheless clearly that of Marx. It is largely because of this style that he has managed to draw so many curious readers further into the pages of the pamphlet. In the single-page preamble which precedes the titled main sections of the *Manifesto*, and with which the present commentary begins, he employed that characteristic style with gusto.

The preamble

Marx's preamble is in fact a far more significant element of the *Manifesto* than may at first be supposed. The rather whimsical notion of a spectre that is central to the preamble's argument in its three short paragraphs may appear to be merely inessential rhetoric that prepares the way for the main argument. While it does indeed present some introductory rhetoric, this was nevertheless very cleverly designed by its author to tempt readers to delve into the main sections. Such rhetoric, moreover, actually contributes to a very powerful ploy to encourage the readers to engage in a political campaign. The pamphlet is, after all, a manifesto in purpose as well as in name – a manifesto being, as Osborne has usefully summarized, 'a performance, which uses language to enact a will to realize a particular future'.[5]

To grasp fully the significance of Marx's preamble and also of the ploy for which it is a vehicle, one needs to be aware that among his favourite literary tactics was the use of metaphorical speech.[6] In the very first sentence one finds a clear example of his mastery of this tactic whereby he introduces the spectre. 'A spectre is haunting Europe', he wrote, 'the spectre of Communism' (p. 73). That he was indeed speaking metaphorically rather than expressing a genuine belief in the supernatural is quite obvious if one considers the remainder of the paragraph carefully. 'All the powers of old Europe', he went on, 'have entered into a holy alliance to exorcise this spectre: Pope and Czar, Metternich and Guizot, French Radicals and German police-spies' (p. 73). Marx was not, of course, saying that all these powerful people were actually trying literally to exorcise what they really believed to be a genuine spectre or ghost that was haunting people in the continent of Europe. He was, rather, ridiculing the attempts of the holders of vested interests, pursued along with other reactionaries in the existing society, to scare people away from having any yearning or even, indeed, sympathy for communism.

The term 'spectre' had actually been used for such a purpose by the opponents of communism earlier in the 1840s. The doctrine of communism was indeed portrayed in that period in such a way as to frighten people who might have been tempted to subscribe to it.[7] This very real effort to strike fear was being undertaken by means of what, according to Moore's translation, Marx called a 'nursery tale of the Spectre of Communism' (p. 73). Now, in his alternative, far more recent translation of the *Manifesto* Carver suggests that Marx meant horror stories rather than nursery tales.[8] Nevertheless, this does not affect the argument as such stories and tales usually have in common an element of absurdity designed to terrify readers.

Marx was thus indeed demonstrating from the outset the absurdity of the type of response that he expected the *Manifesto* would face from those who had reasons to try to oppose it and ensure the maintenance of the existing society. For this purpose he was employing a method known widely by philosophers as *reductio ad absurdum* (reduction to absurdity). This method, which is actually simpler than it may sound, involves the attempt to substantiate one's own argument by revealing the opposing thesis to be false or absurd. This is achieved by exposing that other thesis as nonsense. By employing the metaphor of the spectre, Marx wanted to demonstrate that communism would be the most rational option for society to take. In order for opponents to prove communism not to be so, they had often sought to depict it as something evil. An effective way to do this would, as mentioned above, be to devise something akin to a nursery tale (or horror story). Because such a fictional story, a key purpose of which is to frighten children or adults, will include the element of absurdity, those who have been initially scared are often later embarrassed. If this is the best that opponents can do in order to portray communism as the opposite of a good option, then the argument that communism is indeed the best option will be strengthened significantly.

Taking what is perhaps an amusing aside, it is interesting to note that an early English language edition of the *Manifesto*, translated by Helen Macfarlane and published in 1850, had mistakenly said 'frightful hobgoblin' rather than 'spectre'. This translation is less accurate than 'spectre' which, as mentioned earlier, was approved by Engels. Nevertheless, 'frightful hobgoblin' does, as Paul Thomas has suggested, invoke the tales of Hans Christian Anderson and the Brothers Grimm who were very popular in the 1840s. Perhaps the term 'frightful hobgoblin' would have served very well Marx's intention to persuade those who believed the criticism thus presented against communism that they should grow up.[9] What is most significant, however, is that each of these translations – 'frightful hobgoblin' and 'spectre' – illustrates the attempt to frighten people, and in both cases alike the attempt can be shown to be absurd.

Once one recognizes that he was using such mischievous tactics, it becomes plain to see that Marx was seeking to grasp his readers' attention by mocking the portrayal of communism as a spectre. The forces of reaction had needed to create this story of the spectre to frighten both themselves and others. A more sensible, critical analysis on the part of those forces would, as Carver has suggested, have been unlikely to have achieved its objective. This apparition of the spectre had been used to draw attention away from the problems that the exploited classes were enduring in the existing society and, crucially, to divert those classes from the opportunities that were beginning to emerge for the resolution of those problems by means of fundamental social and political change.[10] Marx, as we have just seen, seized on this use of the spectre metaphor in order to employ it very skilfully for his own purpose. It was, Marx stressed, 'high time that Communists should openly, in the face of the whole world, publish their views, their aims, their tendencies' (p. 73). The *Manifesto* was, as the remainder of this guide will hopefully illustrate, intended to fulfil that purpose by all the means available to him, and without pulling any punches.

Study questions

1 Why did Marx use the metaphor of the spectre?
2 How effective is his use of the spectre metaphor in these early paragraphs?

3 Would 'frightful hobgoblin' have been any better than 'spectre' as a term to convey Marx's message to English-language readers?

4 Does the term 'horror story' that replaces nursery tale in the more recent translation make much difference to the interpretation and presentation of Marx's argument?

5 How useful was his use of the method that philosophers sometimes call *reductio ad absurdum*?

6 Why can 'Manifesto' be considered a very appropriate word in the title of the pamphlet?

'Bourgeois and proletarians'

The first main section of the *Manifesto* gets immediately to its point by beginning with a statement presented in the form of a paragraph comprising only a single sentence. 'The history of all hitherto existing society', Marx announced, 'is the history of class struggles' (p. 74). This statement served at once to link together two of the pamphlet's main themes discussed in the previous chapter of this guide: class struggle and the materialist conception of history. The message Marx was thereby conveying was that the history of society was not primarily of ideas but, rather, of actual struggles, involving material things – including human beings. While the philosophical element of the *Manifesto* was thus set in train by this vitally important sentence, the political purpose of the pamphlet was also being pursued. By so presenting class struggle as the key feature of the process of history he was, in effect, announcing to his proletarian readers and their representatives that activism would be required on their part.

To grasp why Marx intended the two themes of class struggle and the materialist conception of history to run together at the core of the *Manifesto*, it is useful at this point to refer to a brief set of 11 research notes that he had made for himself around 3 years earlier. These notes have since been published many times under the title 'Theses on Feuerbach'. One of the key points in these notes was that in order to appreciate how material or, in other words, actual circumstances underwent change in society it was necessary to understand that such circumstances are manipulated and transformed by people. It was, moreover, crucial to grasp that such circumstances were in part comprised of those very same people. As he put it in the last of the notes, 'The philosophers have only interpreted the world, in various ways; the point is to change it.'[11] This perspective of the world helped shape the views of Marx and Engels when, by means of their joint effort, they produced the *Manifesto*. What Marx was stressing was that if the world was really to be changed then class struggle would be necessary.

Marx continued in the *Manifesto* by identifying a range of groups, which he described as classes, each of which had in some period since the days of ancient Rome been involved in the struggles. Those struggles were in each case against the oppression of one or more class by another. The results of the struggles were either the common ruin of all those involved or a 'revolutionary reconstitution of society' (p. 74), which in turn involved further such struggles. The use of the word 'revolutionary' is significant in that it continued to represent and amplify the dynamism and extent of change in this process that Marx sought to illustrate.

This history of class struggles had, Marx suggested, culminated in the struggle he was experiencing between the bourgeoisie and the proletariat. This latest struggle was, like its predecessors, characterized by antagonism and oppression. It was, nevertheless, in another, fundamental way a rather different struggle. The sense of temporal changeability he had started to convey is maintained by means of his statement that this new struggle had begun to take place in the 'modern bourgeois society that has sprouted from the ruins of feudal society' (p. 74). It is here that he introduced another of the main themes, this being the epoch of the bourgeoisie. A feature of this epoch that set it apart from all the previous ones he had just mentioned was that the class antagonisms by which it was characterized had been simplified significantly. 'Society as a whole', he argued, was 'more and more splitting up into two great hostile camps, into two great classes directly facing each other: Bourgeoisie and Proletariat' (pp. 74–5).

Marx began at this point to outline the processes whereby, first, the bourgeoisie had risen to become the dominant class and, second, the proletariat had emerged as the class that would bring about the end of such dominance. For this purpose he adopted and adapted the dialectical method that, as was mentioned in Chapter one of the present guide, Hegel had pioneered. Before progressing further into the *Manifesto* it will, hence, be useful to focus briefly on that method once again.

In his interpretation of the dialectic Hegel had, as we have seen, presented his argument that in the historical process the human mind first interprets the world, second rethinks that interpretation by developing increasingly sophisticated concepts and third, as a result, overcomes the problems of earlier interpretations. Marx employed the dialectic method very differently to argue that the historical process was not fundamentally one of thought but, rather, one of action. Perhaps the best way to grasp Marx's use of the method, and the way in which it differed from that of Hegel, is to turn to the well-known Postface he wrote to the second German edition of his major work *Capital, Volume One* in 1873.

In the Postface, Marx declared that his dialectical method was the exact opposite to that of Hegel who had portrayed the process by which the human brain did its thinking as an independent subject that created the real world. Hegel had called this apparently independent subject the Idea. 'With me', Marx stressed, 'the reverse is true: the ideal is nothing but the material world reflected in the mind of man, and translated into forms of thought.'[12] The real, material world was thus, for Marx, the principal force. In Hegel's attempt to apply it to the process of history the dialectic was 'standing on its head'. Hence, Marx went on, 'it must be inverted, in order to discover the rational kernel within the mystical shell'.[13] The dialectic would thus be concerned primarily with processes in the material world.

Turning back to the *Manifesto* one can see that Marx was indeed applying the dialectical method in a materialist manner. The bourgeoisie, he argued, created new means and patterns of producing and distributing goods, and the administration thereof. In this process humans overcame the less-developed means and patterns of old which had tendencies that posed what he described in this and some of his other works as contradictions to the newly developing ones.[14]

In such terms the dialectical process was such that the epoch of the bourgeoisie was characterized by a series of such contradictions.[15] This notion of contradiction helps clarify the philosophical significance of what may at first seem like a very simple descriptive narrative in this section of the pamphlet. Contradictions sometimes emerge in logic in cases where two propositions are stated. There is a contradiction when the status of one of those propositions as true must deem the other to be false. Marx conceived of contradictions in material terms.[16] They emerged when one condition, such as domination by a group or class, made another condition, such as the success of another group or class, untenable. This clash occurred because of the very nature of the connection between the two conditions.[17]

The epoch of the bourgeoisie can itself be seen in terms of a broader contradiction with which Marx was concerned in the *Manifesto*. This was a contradiction that could be seen between, on the one hand, the continuation of an outdated mode of production and, on the other hand, the development of productive forces. He would in 1859 emphasize this particular contradiction in the passage of the 'Preface to *A Critique of Political Economy*' which, as was mentioned in Chapter two of this guide, he described as the guiding thread. It was, he declared, a thread that ran through the various works, including the *Manifesto*, in which Engels and he had hitherto presented their views. Hence, it is worthwhile to turn yet again to that guiding thread as presented in 1859 for his summary of the way in which this contradiction has to be overcome: 'No social order ever perishes', the thread states, 'before all the productive forces for which there is room in it have developed; and new higher relations of production never appear before the material conditions of their existence have matured in the womb of the old society itself'.[18] In the *Manifesto* he had been suggesting that these were processes that society was in fact experiencing.

Some of the historical conditions that Marx discussed in the *Manifesto* can thus be understood in terms of material contradictions that were played out within that of the epoch of the bourgeoisie. Marx started by outlining the broad contradiction that came about with the spread of the rising bourgeoisie around the world, including the expansion of its power into the Americas, India and China. The old feudal system of industry, where closed guilds dominated industrial production, could not produce the goods that were needed to provide for the huge scale of the newly growing markets. This contradiction was resolved by the continuation of bourgeois expansion and the subsequent decline of feudalism. As a result, the system in which the guilds had helped distribute labour was replaced by a division of labour in each workshop (p. 75).

To grasp fully the point of what Marx was saying at this stage in the *Manifesto* one needs a little knowledge of the guild system that had emerged and flourished in medieval times. The guilds of particular trades, which were organized in each guild town or city, monopolized production. Licences that could be bought only from the lords were necessary in order for people to become members of any of these guilds. There were limits to how many people could actually purchase such licences as they were expensive and, moreover, restricted in availability.

As part of the process of the decline of feudalism the rising bourgeoisie began to build factories outside the traditional guild towns and thus beyond the restrictions of the guild system. The guilds thereby lost their monopolies. Furthermore, craftsmen, unlike their predecessors within the guilds, no longer created objects in their entirety. Workers instead performed roles in workshops where, monotonously, they made the same contributions to objects over again, while other workers performed similar roles until the whole objects were complete. While this was a far more productive process, which made the capitalists who owned the factories much more money, workers suffered what Marx in some of his writings prior to the *Manifesto* had described as alienation from their work, from their products and from their fellow human beings. These alienated workers of the new system comprised the proletarian class which, as we saw in the earlier chapters of this guide, was central to Marx's concerns.[19]

Marx went on in the *Manifesto* to detail how the economic and political power of the bourgeoisie had grown rapidly as the industrial revolution progressed, culminating in what later became known as the epoch of dual revolution that straddled the feudal epoch and that of the bourgeoisie. The epoch of dual revolution was, as was mentioned earlier in this guide, characterized by industrial and political change that was both fast and fundamental. Thinking back momentarily to the situation a few hundred years earlier, Marx remarked that the discovery of America had paved way for modern industry to establish the world market. This market had brought about great developments in international commerce, navigation and communications. These developments in turn provided the conditions for the expansion of industry and the rapid and extensive geographical growth of the railways. The bourgeoisie was thus able to increase its own capital, while all other classes which had managed since the Middle Ages until now to maintain some economic power were weakened. Those other classes were, as Marx put it, 'pushed into the background'. 'We see', he went on, 'how the modern bourgeoisie is itself the product of a long course of development, of a series of revolutions in the modes of production and of exchange' (p. 75). This historical development can be seen in terms of the dialectical process whereby a number of contradictions were being resolved leading to new ones. All this took place within the broader contradiction of the epoch of the bourgeoisie that, Marx hoped, would eventually be resolved just like the rest.

At this point in the text, however, Marx was not yet ready to discuss the possibility of putting an end to this broader contradiction. This would be something that would be dealt with later in the pamphlet. First, the narrative of the *Manifesto* turned to the consequences of the economic developments that had increased bourgeois power. 'Each step in the development of the bourgeoisie was', he argued, 'accompanied by a corresponding political advance of that class' (p. 75). He outlined the series of different relationships within which the bourgeoisie had been involved. From being oppressed by the feudal nobility, through alliances with various types of monarchy in order to counter the power of the nobility, the bourgeoisie had eventually achieved the industrial, economic and commercial dominance that now assured it what he called 'exclusive political sway' (p. 76) in the modern representative state. By 'sway' Marx meant control. Indeed, the wording of Carver's translation is 'exclusive political control'.[20] This, of course, was a very broad generalization, skimming over various sorts of relationships in a range of countries at different times within these wide-ranging categories; but in a political pamphlet such as the *Manifesto* the point was to offer a general summary rather than a detailed account such as one finds in some of his other, more substantial works.

Marx went on to make the following, equally bold generalization: 'The executive of the modern state is but a committee for managing the common affairs of the whole bourgeoisie' (p. 76). This provocative statement raises the question whether Marx really believed that the dominant class was a monolithic and thus undivided bourgeoisie. It is unlikely that he and Engels, being as they were thinkers who studied the details of society in very close detail, would actually believe this to be the case.

Indeed, that Marx understood clearly that the bourgeoisie was not monolithic may perhaps be substantiated by considering a crucial word in the sentence just quoted: 'committee'. If the executive of the state is to be considered as such, then an important point is that committees act with some autonomy from the members they represent.[21] Some of the interests of different segments of the bourgeoisie, moreover, are likely to conflict with one another, and the state may sacrifice those of one segment or more to those interests which are shared by all such segments.[22] The latter interests are those of the common affairs which, as Marx mentioned in this controversial sentence, are to be managed. His point was that, even though there were different and conflicting interests within the ruling class, there were nevertheless some broader interests that all the members of that class held in common with one another.

Returning to Carver's translation for a moment one finds, however, that the question whether Marx considered the bourgeoisie to be monolithic might not be resolved quite so clearly. According to this translation the sentence we have been considering says: 'The power of the state is merely a device for administrating the common affairs of the whole bourgeoisie'.[23] Now a 'device' does not necessarily have the autonomy of a 'committee'. Nevertheless, the stress on common interests rather than a single interest is still there. Of course, this is rather more tenuous than is the case in the Moore translation. Because of this discrepancy it is perhaps appropriate to provide further verification of his understanding of the bourgeoisie as less than monolithic. This can be found in a sentence a few pages later (to which we return in a different context shortly) where according to the Moore version Marx stressed that, in its struggle against exploitation by the capitalist class, the proletariat 'compels legislative recognition of particular interests of the workers, by taking advantage of the divisions among the bourgeoisie itself' (p. 82). In the case of this sentence Carver's slightly different translation actually helps confirm that Marx did not see the bourgeoisie as monolithic. The proletariat, according to the Carver version, 'compels the recognition of workers' individual interests in legal form by taking advantage of divisions within the bourgeoisie itself'.[24] The divided bourgeoisie appears in each of these translations, and a divided bourgeoisie is, of course, not a monolithic one.

As Marx's discussion of the way in which the bourgeoisie achieved sway continues, one finds him reminding his readers that the approach of the bourgeoisie in this phase of history had actually been revolutionary. He then elaborated on this point with a couple of comments. We might understand these comments more clearly by means of the references in the next few paragraphs of this guide to a few works he wrote, and to some experiences he had before and after he wrote the *Manifesto*.

In the first of these two comments Marx said that wherever it had gained the upper hand the bourgeoisie had 'put an end to all feudal, patriarchal, idyllic relations' and 'pitilessly torn asunder the motley feudal ties that bound man to his "natural superiors"' (p. 76). It may appear that Marx was switching from an issue about the political executive to one regarding the more fundamental relations of production without any real structure to hold the discussion together. By taking another look, however, at Marx's guiding thread in the 'Preface to *A Critique of Political Economy*' we can see that by reading such a switch into the text one would miss something very significant. Bearing in mind the guiding thread one can see how this point regarding relations in society, which he portrayed so dramatically, may be linked to the statement discussed earlier that the state is the executive committee of the bourgeoisie. In the guiding thread he stated that, in the course of social production, people entered into 'relations of production which correspond to a definite stage of the development of their material productive forces'. On these relations of production which may be portrayed as 'the economic structure of society' there was built 'a legal and political superstructure'.[25] This superstructure would, in the general political terms we use today, be called the state. As relations of production are transformed by the growing economic power of the bourgeoisie, this situation is reflected in political power, which is asserted through the executive of the modern state. The economic and political aspects of power were thus in his view related to one another.

Marx continued in the *Manifesto* by stating, in the second of the comments with which we are concerned here, that the bourgeoisie had 'left remaining no other nexus between man and man than naked self-interest, than callous "cash payment"' (p. 76). This should be read with his point about the breaking of motley feudal ties in mind. There were no such ties powerful enough to keep this nexus within bounds. The bourgeois class had, he went on in his elaborate prose, 'drowned the most heavenly ecstasies of religious fervour, of chivalrous enthusiasm, of philistine sentimentalism, in the icy water of egotistical calculation' (p. 76). That class had 'resolved personal worth into exchange value' (p. 76). To grasp what Marx was trying to communicate in this passage we need first to focus briefly on what he had written in some of his earlier works about alienation. This will shed some light on his point about resolving personal worth into exchange value. It will also help if we consider for a moment the theory of value that he was beginning to develop, and which would become a major feature of his later work.

Before turning to Marx's theory of value let us recap on some earlier discussion in this guide about his theory of alienation: in Marx's view people suffer from this condition when they are denied the fruits of their labour, when the things they produce come to dominate them, and when they thus are in effect estranged from their species-being or, in other words, from their human nature. As he discussed in detail in the 'Economic and Social Manuscripts' of 1844, this happens when those products are valued only in terms of the money they are deemed to be worth in the market. Subsequently, the human labour which created the products is itself considered as nothing but a commodity to be sold and bought in the market. This consideration becomes institutionalized by the social and economic institutions of society. Institutionalization results in barely questioned acceptance of this process. One thing that is thereby overlooked is that humans naturally produce in cooperation with their fellows. The people who make or contribute to the making of things come to perceive them as alien objects. Hence, in this very egoistic environment they actually become alienated from their fellows and indeed from their species-being, which is a social being.[26] As this process takes place those humans who exploit others are themselves dehumanized because of their actions which are incompatible with the cooperation of the species-being. This serves to illustrate that Marx held a distinctive conception of human nature. As Norman Geras has suggested, this conception continued to be a feature of Marx's thought.[27]

The concept of human nature helps clarify the continuity which, because of some significant changes in the terms Marx used, can be difficult to detect. By the time he came to write the *Manifesto* Marx had refrained from using the terms 'alienation' and 'species-being', not least because of some incisive criticism by the individualist/

egoist philosopher Max Stirner, who stressed that such terms had religious and metaphysical connotations.[28] Nevertheless, Marx did not abandon the philosophy that lay beneath the terms. The limitation of personal worth to exchange value with which Marx was concerned in the *Manifesto* can thus be seen in terms of alienation. Personal worth was far richer than value for the sake of oneself as an individual. By nature humans considered their worth to have a social aspect. As is indicated by the passage quoted earlier about the drowning of the most heavenly ecstasies of religious fervour and other qualities, he believed that the process leading to the condition of alienation involved the substitution of exchange value for the recognition of such worth.

What Marx meant by exchange value can be discerned if one turns to a series of lectures he delivered in Brussels the year before the *Manifesto* appeared in print. He intended to publish the lectures in Brussels in February 1848; but the revolutionary uprisings of that time delayed this until the following year. When they did appear it was as a set of newspaper articles in the *Neue Rheinische Zeitung*, with added reference at the beginning to the events of 1848. The articles were eventually modified and put together by Engels in 1891 to form the pamphlet *Wage-Labour and Capital*. David McLellan includes in his selection of Marx's works a translation that follows the original text of the newspaper articles. This is useful for the purposes of this guide as we are concerned with what Marx meant in 1848. Hence, it is that translation that is referenced here.

'The workers', Marx argued in those articles, 'exchange their commodity, labour, for the commodity of the capitalist, and this exchange takes place in a definite ratio'.[29] This ratio was a certain amount of money for a certain amount of labour. 'The exchange value of a commodity', he added, 'reckoned in money, is what is called its price'.[30] In order to subsist and perhaps enjoy some basic pleasures the workers sold their labour to the capitalist as a commodity. Being thus merely something to be sold, work was not considered by those workers to be a manifestation of their lives. Life, on the contrary, was perceived to begin after work was finished; work for the worker was simply that which gained earnings, 'which bring him to the table, to the public house, to bed'.[31]

The cost of the production of labour was merely such money that was required as wages to maintain, develop and reproduce workers as workers. As soon as those workers consumed the means of subsistence future use of such means was lost to them. The workers were, in other words, unable to use those means in order to create new values in their place. It is, Marx explained, 'this noble reproductive power that the worker surrenders to the capitalist in exchange for means of subsistence received'.[32] The relevance of all this for the brief comment in the *Manifesto* on resolving personal worth into exchange value seems to be verified if we turn to Engels' answer to Question 5 of 'Principles of Communism'. This, readers will remember, served as one of the drafts of the *Manifesto*. There Engels described labour as a commodity and condemned wages as being restricted to the means of subsistence and reproduction of the working class.[33] The newspaper articles that would later be revised to form *Wage-Labour and Capital* hence throw some light on this brief part of the text in the *Manifesto*.

As can be discerned from this brief look at some of Marx and Engels' other writings, their view was that capitalists benefited from exchanges with the workers by gaining all the value from the production process other than that which those workers received in wages to keep them alive and perhaps enjoy some minimal, basic pleasure. In the process, workers and capitalists alike had suffered what Marx had in his early work referred to as alienation.

When one's attention reverts back to the passage in the *Manifesto* that prompted the present discussion, Marx, it will be seen, stressed that many chartered freedoms that had been considered as fixed, and enjoyed permanently depending on one's place in society before the epoch of bourgeois dominance, had been lost. This meant that the old means by which people had been exploited by other people who enjoyed dominant positions in society were beginning to disappear. The fact that poor people had some worth as human beings with parts to play in society was recognized in the feudal era, even though patriarchy and the condescension on the part of the dominant serve to indicate that human equality was not. Even these limited notions of personal worth were in demise along with those earlier means of exploitation. In their place, he went on, the bourgeoisie had set up a single freedom unrestrained by conscience. This new freedom was that of 'Free Trade' (p. 76), which had become a doctrine whereby the bourgeoisie could avoid measures such as tariffs and protectionist levies.[34] In Carver's translation there is the extra word 'conscienceless' before 'free trade'. This extra word makes Marx's view of the bourgeoisie in this respect still more clearly evident.[35]

The brief mention of free trade in the *Manifesto* helps situate Marx's thought within his political, social and intellectual environment. Indeed, some key historical events had helped shape the views he was expressing in the pamphlet. In 1846, the Corn Law, which removed tariffs, had been introduced in England. Supporters of the law suggested that it would lead to lower prices and greater consumption, subsequently leading to increased production and more people in work for higher pay. Marx, on the other hand, speaking in Belgium at the Brussels Democratic Association in January 1848 (a month during which he was finishing the *Manifesto*), said that this would be unlikely to be the result. This was because, as had already been the case in Britain in recent decades, capital would be accumulated by the increased use of machinery meaning greater exploitation and deeper poverty both for workers in the capitalist countries and for the people abroad whose lives were ruined by the expansion of the bourgeois mode of production. Nevertheless, free trade had the progressive function of enabling this capitalist mode to develop to the fullest extent possible before its demise. Hence, Marx declared, not entirely ironically, that he was in favour of free trade.[36] He published the speech as a pamphlet the following month. After presenting an argument that both protectionism and free trade work against the proletariat he said, 'the free trade system hastens the social revolution'. It was, he went on, 'in this revolutionary sense alone that I vote in favour of free trade'.[37]

This focus on Marx's brief mention of free trade in both negative and positive terms helps illustrate another feature at the end of the passage in the *Manifesto* with which we have been concerned in some detail in the previous few paragraphs. This feature is the beginning of a narrative in which Marx switches between exploitative and progressive aspects of the rise of the bourgeoisie. At this point Marx makes a comment that helps illustrate the combination of each of these two aspects: 'for exploitation, veiled by religious and political illusions, [the bourgeoisie] has substituted naked, shameless, direct, brutal exploitation' (p. 76). On the one hand, Marx saw exploitation in terms of unpaid surplus labour being extracted by one class from people in another class.[38] Nevertheless, on the other hand, as an atheist he would from another angle have been rather pleased to see the passing of religious doctrines that held back human enlightenment and development. The predominantly egoistical society with its inherent exploitation was, however, not for him an attractive prospect. As will be discussed shortly, for him such a society would need to be abolished in the next stage of the broader dialectical process; but the progressive features would be retained as the building of a new society followed the demise of the capitalist mode of production.

After the passage regarding exploitation, quoted above, Marx continued this narrative of the exploitative and progressive features of the rise of the bourgeoisie. First, each of a range of previously honoured and revered professions had been 'stripped of its halo' or, in other words, stripped of its reputation for good motives, as those who were or might have become members of those professions became 'paid wage labourers' (p. 76). Of course, not every member of the professions he listed – physicians, lawyers, priests, poets and scientists – left their positions to become actual labourers in the terms that we usually understand the word 'labourer' today. What Marx actually meant can be grasped with reference to his guiding thread in the 'Preface to *A Critique of Political Economy*'. There he said that the superstructure that was built on the economic foundations was dominated by the ideas of the exploiting class. These ideas permeate throughout society and come to be represented by the majority of the members of professions whose work is guided by them. Hence, the term 'paid workforce' in Carver's translation of the *Manifesto* in place of 'paid wage labourers' seems to present Marx's message more satisfactorily.[39]

Marx went on in the *Manifesto* to stress that even the family had become dominated by the cash nexus. The bourgeoisie had, he complained, 'torn away from the family its sentimental veil, and has reduced the family relation to a mere money relation' (p. 76). As will be mentioned shortly in the present discussion, he returned later in the pamphlet to the ways in which members of the bourgeoisie themselves acted in this respect. Regarding the effects upon the working class, however, this point about the mere money relation is concerned with the necessity for all members of the family, including young children, to go out to work in order to bring in the means of subsistence.

As Marx switched abruptly to the broader developments, the productive forces that were central to his argument were clearly evident. Marx stressed that as the industrial revolution progressed the bourgeoisie which drove it forward had 'accomplished wonders far surpassing Egyptian pyramids, Roman aqueducts and Gothic cathedrals' (p. 76). The industrial revolution had also brought about huge developments in transportation and thereby, Marx went on, the bourgeoisie had 'conducted expeditions that put in the shade all former Exoduses of nations and crusades' (p. 76). Although he did not elaborate on the latter point, this was the age of imperialism which involved the migration from and to the colonies. Of course, although Marx did not mention it, this was forceful migration in the case of migration from those locations. Although there had been a brutal display of vigour in the middle ages, this had been complemented by 'the most slothful indolence' (p. 76) which had become a thing of the past.

At this point in the text the narrative of the *Manifesto* begins to place greater emphasis upon the demise that, Marx believed, the bourgeoisie would soon undergo. Marx stressed that the bourgeoisie could maintain its existence only by 'constantly revolutionising the instruments of production, and thereby the relations of production, and with them the whole relations of society' (p. 77). This was in contrast to earlier industrial classes which had needed to conserve the modes of production in which they operated. Those earlier classes had indeed required the very opposite of the constant revolutionizing of production and subsequently of all other aspects of society. As the old relations which had been considered permanent were swept away, so was the respect for their prejudices and opinions. New relations were, moreover, replaced before they had time to develop differences within themselves. Marx summed up this swift process of change with a comment that has traditionally received the following, notoriously vague translation: 'All that is solid melts into air' (p. 77). The mental image of a fast process of vapourization that is thus generated does create a sense of the temporary nature of each situation as the dialectic takes its course at a rapid pace. One gains a better picture of what he meant, however, by turning to Carver's more accurate translation. 'All that is solid melts into air' is replaced with: 'Everything feudal and fixed goes up in smoke.'[40] It is clear in this translation that he continues to discuss the demise of feudalism.

Having skilfully planted the image of the disappearance of feudalism firmly in the minds of his readers, Marx turned his attention and theirs back to the international aspect of the speedy development of the capitalist epoch. In order to find new markets and thus continue its operations and indeed its very existence, the bourgeois system needed to spread around the world and indeed was doing so, as he had mentioned earlier in the pamphlet. Once again he was identifying what he considered as progressive tendencies along with the maintenance of the old exploitative ones in an uneasy relationship within the dialectical process. The bourgeoisie had 'through its exploitation of the world-market given a cosmopolitan character to production and consumption in every country' (p. 77). The reactionaries of society whose economic power rested on a seemingly permanent basis had thus been alarmed to see that industry was no longer organized on the national boundaries of old. The new industries that had taken the place of those that had thus fallen no longer relied on raw materials from the territories in which they were based but, rather, drew such materials from locations all around the world. New wants had been encouraged which could be satisfied only by products from such distant parts of the globe. This had brought about a system of international interdependence involving not just material production but also the production and propagation of ideas. The progressive element is here prominent: 'National one-sidedness and narrow-mindedness become more and more impossible, and from the numerous national and local literatures there arises a world literature' (p. 77).

This allusion in the narrative of the *Manifesto* to a progressive aspect was immediately followed by a discussion of an exploitative one, in which Marx criticized Western aggression. In the latter case, however, his words expressed the Western-centrist, patronizing and thus what would today in some quarters be called Orientalist nature of accepted knowledge in his intellectual environment. The rapid developments and improvements in production and communication brought about by the bourgeoisie had drawn 'all, even the most barbarian, nations into civilisation' (p. 77). The low prices of the commodities produced under the control of the bourgeoisie were, he stressed in a metaphor-strewn sentence, 'the heavy artillery with which it batters down all Chinese walls, with which it forces the barbarians' intensely obstinate hate of foreigners to capitulate' (p. 77).

What Marx meant by 'Chinese walls' needs a little attention in order to clarify the point he was trying to convey. Such clarification has become particularly important today as the term is used now often to refer to conceptual barriers between groups. The way in which Marx was using the term was indeed conceptual, based on the failure to prevent Western exploitation which involved the export of cheaply produced goods. What, however, makes the point particularly effective for Marx, with his tendency to seek for opportunities to devise metaphors, was that of course China did (and does) have its famous, ancient protective wall. The Chinese walls metaphor was, thus, effective in another way too. The failure of China to restrict imports served as an excellent example with which to show resistance to the capitalist onslaught to be futile, its great wall proving to be useless in this case. Yet another reason why the sentence worked so well is that its metaphor of heavy artillery reflected the real use of heavy weaponry that had been used in the Opium War – a war that was still very recent history at the time the *Manifesto* was published – which had opened the way for the flood of cheap goods into China.

To throw still more light on Marx's use of the term 'Chinese walls' it is useful to turn once again to Engels' second draft: 'Principles of Communism'. In his answer to Question 11 of this draft's catechism he outlined in far more plain terms than Marx tended to use the situation regarding China: 'We have come to the point where a new machine invented in England today deprives millions of Chinese workers their livelihood within a year's time.'[41] All the people in the world had, he went on, because of large-scale industry been brought together into contact with one another. Small local markets had been merged into one world market. In the same Eurocentric tone as Marx after him, however, he said that large-scale industry had 'spread civilization and progress everywhere and has thus ensured that whatever happens in the civilized countries will have repercussions in all other countries'.[42]

Turning back to the 'Chinese walls' passage in the *Manifesto*, we find Marx saying that all nations were compelled to adopt the bourgeois mode of production. Now, in a sentence which indicates that he used the term barbarian and civilization with an element of irony earlier in the paragraph, he said the bourgeoisie compelled all other nations 'to introduce what it calls civilization' (pp. 77–8): the significant words here were 'what it calls'. The bourgeoisie thus, he went on, 'creates a world after its own image' (p. 78).

While he added this element of irony at this point in the *Manifesto*, Marx did nevertheless once again use the term 'barbarian' in a patronizing sense in the next paragraph, where he said barbarian and semi-barbarian countries had become dependent on the civilized ones – 'the East on the West' (p. 78). At the national level, returning to the demographic change he had mentioned earlier, he said that the huge new cities and towns were dominating the country and power in the representative systems had begun to reflect such change. A positive aspect of these developments was that the bourgeoisie had thus 'rescued a considerable part of the population from the idiocy of rural life' (p. 78). Such isolated progressive results of bourgeois dominance were, as will be discussed further, in Marx's view, all contributing to the future downfall of the dominant class.

Notwithstanding the steadily growing and immanent problems for the bourgeoisie, its own power continued to grow. Just as the populace was becoming more and more centralized, Marx went on, so too were property, the means of production and therefore politics. This served the class interest of the bourgeoisie as previously semi-autonomous provinces now came in each country to have one code of laws, one customs tariff and a single taxation system (p. 78).

As has been observed at a number of points so far in this guide, the processes of change were, for Marx, driven by productive forces. At this stage, for the first time in the *Manifesto*, he focused directly on those forces. They had grown more rapidly during the period of the rise of the bourgeoisie than in all previous eras. This involved 'subjection of Nature's forces to man, machinery, application of chemistry to industry and agriculture, steam-navigation, railways, electric telegraphs, clearing of whole continents for cultivation, canalisation of rivers, whole populations conjured out of the ground' (p. 78).

As one considers this brief comment by Marx about the productive forces, the grounds for his later comment in the 'Preface to *A Critique of Political Economy*', that the guiding thread he presented in that work had been in part formulated in the *Manifesto*, become very clear. The dialectical nature of the process that Marx perceived is, moreover, very apparent. As the forces began to develop in feudal society, he argued, the particular means of production were generated which became the foundations of bourgeois power. As those means of production became more firmly established there came a point at which feudal methods in agriculture and industry could no longer accommodate the productive forces in the advanced stage they had reached. Feudal relations of production became the fetters of the productive forces. Those feudal relations 'had to be burst asunder; they were burst asunder' (p. 78). In another sentence that indicates still further that he did not assume that the bourgeois class was monolithic, Marx stressed that in the place of feudal society free competition had been generated by the social and political constitution under 'the economic and political sway of the bourgeois class' (p. 78). The political sway of this dominant class thus allowed for competition among its members – competition implying a pluralistic rather than monolithic composition of that class. Marx's discussion of the rise of the bourgeoisie comes to its end at this point. It does so with the following short sentence that serves, on the one hand, to terminate the flow of the narrative on the rise of this class and, on the other hand, to open a new paragraph to mark the beginning of a new phase: 'A similar movement is going on before our own eyes' (p. 78).

The first main section of the *Manifesto* on the relations between bourgeois and proletarians is from this point onwards concerned with two main expectations. First, there was the potential for the demise of the bourgeoisie to accelerate. Second was the development of the power of the proletariat and its ability to lead a revolution that would replace capitalism with a new society. These two factors would represent similar processes to those of the fall of feudalism and rise of the bourgeoisie, with which Marx had been concerned until this point in the pamphlet. He had, indeed, said that the foundations of bourgeois power had been generated in feudal society. It was under feudalism that the early stages of the industrial revolution began as the productive forces were fostered and harnessed. At the point at which feudalism was becoming a fetter on those forces because its vested interest would be threatened by further development, feudal relations were burst asunder. Capitalist relations would similarly be burst asunder.

In what is one of the most striking and memorable sentences of the *Manifesto* Marx predicted that the capitalist society would not be able for ever to accommodate the development of productive forces. In that sentence, once again using an otherworldly metaphor, he warned that, having 'conjured up such gigantic means of production and exchange' modern bourgeois society was 'like the sorcerer, who is no longer able to control the powers of the nether world whom he has called up by his spells' (pp. 78–79). The existence of the bourgeoisie and its rule now depended on the ability to hold back the forces of production. This was illustrated, he said, by the periodic crises through which capitalism had to proceed. Each time that this had happened a quantity of products, along with the productive forces that had created them, had to be destroyed in order to delay further development of those forces.

Marx said that in such crises an epidemic breaks out 'that, in all earlier epochs would have seemed an absurdity – the epidemic of overproduction' (p. 79). In the Carver translation one finds 'paradox' in place of 'absurdity'.[43] Carver's version thus portrays Marx's intentions very well, as Marx was actually employing the tactic of paradox in order to illustrate the absurdity of the situation. A paradox involves the use of conflicting propositions, each of which seems true even though the truth of one requires the other to be false. In this instance the situation appeared to be characterized by 'a state of momentary barbarism' in which 'a famine, a universal war of devastation had cut off the supply of every means of subsistence' (p. 79). Why, he posed the question, did industry and commerce seem to have been destroyed? In reply he proffered the following answer: 'Because there is too much civilisation, too much means of subsistence, too much industry, too much commerce' (p. 79).

One of the assumptions in the paradox Marx thus constructed is that there is barbarism in a situation which seemed like famine because products could not be bought, a consequence of this being an economic crisis that had cut off the supply of the very means of subsistence. The other assumption of the paradox was that there was too much with which to provide for subsistence. As a paradox, however, there must be a solution and in this case it is that the second of these assumptions was false, even though it appeared to be real. If it had not been false then there would not have been too much because too much more than sufficient for the purpose; hence, if there were to be more than sufficient resources then that could not be the reason why people are unable to buy enough products to maintain the situation in which commerce and industry avoid failure.

The real reason for the situation that brought about this paradoxical state of affairs was that the productive forces that could have been made available to provide subsistence no longer served the vested interests of the society. In other words, the productive forces, if allowed to develop further, would make redundant the exploitative processes that served the interests of bourgeois property. The productive forces, which had in fact become too powerful for the conditions of bourgeois property, were for this reason now being fettered. At this point in the *Manifesto* the revolutionary potential of the productive forces comes clearly into view: 'so soon as they overcome these fetters, they bring disorder into the whole of bourgeois society, endanger the existence of bourgeois property' (p. 79).

To gain a fuller picture of what, in Marx's view, the situation was like in capitalist society it is useful to consider in very broad and simple terms what may happen if the capitalist mode of production were indeed to produce an abundance of goods. People who had become wage labourers would be able to afford lots of those goods, the price of which would be low because the more wealthy people would no longer want to buy any more of them. Wage labourers would no longer need to work very many hours at exploitative rates of pay. Capital could not therefore be accumulated. The system could not be sustained.

Capitalism had of course been sustained. The reason for this was that there were ways in which the bourgeoisie were able to overcome such crises. New markets could be found and the older ones exploited even more thoroughly than hitherto. A problem, however, that the capitalists were producing for themselves in taking these other options was, Marx stressed, that in effect they were 'paving the way for more extensive and more destructive crises, and ... diminishing the means whereby crises are prevented' (p. 79). In other words, new markets were not limitless and the more exploitation was pursued the greater was the likelihood that what seemed like overproduction would actually happen.

On the one hand, the people who composed the bourgeoisie were allowing the productive forces to develop insofar as this was necessary to serve their own interests. On the other hand, they were fettering those forces when the accommodation of such development would overcome the scarcity that those interests relied upon. The bourgeoisie was in effect working towards its own demise. This dominant class had, moreover, necessarily created the proletarian class that would refuse to tolerate poverty at the point when productive forces were, potentially, powerful enough to provide an abundance of goods. The bourgeoisie had, to use another of Marx's metaphors, thus created the weapons that would be turned against them. Moreover, encouraging his readers once again subconsciously to envisage the sorcery image that he had earlier created, Marx said that the bourgeoisie had 'called into existence the men who are to wield those weapons . . . the proletarians' (p. 79).

Marx went on to reiterate what he had already said about the conditions of the working class under bourgeois dominance. As capital was developed the condition of the proletariat became worse proportionately. Those people who composed the proletariat had to sell periods of their existence as commodities on the market. Because of this situation the value of their labour fluctuated. Moreover, if they could not sell that labour, members of the proletariat may ultimately not even survive. A description of the proletariat by Engels, in response to his own Question 7 in his first draft – 'Draft of a Communist Confession of Faith' – helps clarify in simple terms the point that Marx was making in rather more stylistic prose. The proletariat, Engels stated, 'is a class of society which lives exclusively by its labour and not on the profit from any kind of capital; that class whose weal and woe, whose life and death, therefore, depend on . . . the fluctuation of competition'.[44]

Returning to the *Manifesto* in its final, published form, one finds Marx stressing that the plight of the people who made up the proletarian class was worsened by the machinery that the bourgeoisie employed and thus by the division of labour, the effect of which was to deskill workers. The worker, Marx suggested, 'becomes an appendage of the machine, and it is only the most simple, most monotonous, and most easily acquired knack, that is required of him' (p. 80). This restricted the cost of labour to almost subsistence. As was discussed earlier, this was something he examined in greater detail in *Wage-Labour and Capital*. The work of the wage labourer became more repulsive as machinery made it repetitive. Furthermore, working hours were thus extended or the speed of the machinery increased so that the wages could match the price of the goods produced, minus the capital that the capitalist gained from the process.

All this went on in the vast factories which, as discussed earlier, overcame the restrictions of the guild system. Marx said in the *Manifesto* that the crowding of workers together made them comparable to soldiers under the command of officers and sergeants (by which it is safe to say he meant managers and foremen). He adopted two levels of analysis to describe the enslavement of the masses of labourers, which enabled him to stress the point of this process. They were, he argued, enslaved on the one level by the bourgeois class and the state that served and defended that class. As this is the broader stage within which individuals operate it can be identified as the structural level. On the other level they were enslaved by, on the one hand, foremen or overlookers and, on the other hand, by the bourgeois manufacturers who employed them. As this level is concerned with actual human beings who were doing observable things it can be identified as the agency level. He also said they were enslaved by the machinery they worked with. Of course, technically it was the owners of the machines (the bourgeois manufacturers) who were responsible for the machine, but portraying the proletariat as being 'daily and hourly enslaved by the machine' was a stylistic tactic that presented his point very powerfully (p. 80). The position of the proletariat became worse still, he suggested, as the bourgeoisie openly admitted that greed was the motive for employing the workers in the present circumstances.

Marx declared that, as the circumstances in the factories he had just been describing became firmly established, equality of wages was introduced. This was not, however, the positive development it may at first appear to be. The equality that emerged was, rather, that which resulted from exploitation. The working-class people were all exploited not only in their jobs but also after work by the bourgeois in other spheres, such as landlords, shopkeepers and pawnbrokers. The proletariat grew as the less than successful people from the dominant class got dragged down into the proletariat, as did peasants and craftsmen.

The *Manifesto* at this point takes an important turn as its author had begun to focus more directly on the future and to write as though that future was in sight. Marx stressed that, from its very appearance on the scene and throughout its various stages of development, the proletariat in a capitalist society was in struggle with the bourgeoisie. The main theme of class struggle thus becomes prominent. More in anticipation than as a report of actual developments, Marx described the stages of the struggle. The process began as individuals dared to resist; then groups in factories took up the fight; members of a trade in a particular place then took up the struggle against the major exploitative bourgeois employer. In all these cases, however, the target was not the bourgeois conditions of production that lay at the heart of the problem but, rather, the instruments of such production. The resistance thus involved destruction as workers sought a return to the pre-capitalist conditions of work.

At this stage in the pamphlet Marx's idea of the dialectical process once again becomes very evident. The workers are described as being scattered, unorganized and in competition with one another for the opportunity to sell their labour. They may, however, taking the form of the proletarian class, be set in motion by the bourgeoisie to campaign against the older, previously dominant classes. The workers do not at this stage 'fight their enemies, but the enemies of their enemies' (p. 81). Those enemies of the bourgeoisie include monarchies and landowners as well as the non-industrial bourgeoisie and the petty bourgeoisie. The workers were thus in this process being simply used by the entire bourgeoisie. As each victory against the other classes is in effect a victory of the bourgeoisie, the power of this capitalist class is further enhanced and entrenched. Why and how the workers allowed themselves to be thus employed is not discussed in the *Manifesto,* and this omission may serve merely to confuse readers today. What needs to be noticed is that the workers in the form of the proletariat were not actually agreeing to fight; the fight itself is yet another of Marx's metaphors. The so-called fight against the enemies of their enemies is one that is engaged in as the bourgeoisie sets up conditions by which the workers are transformed into the proletariat by taking the only opportunities – those of wage labour – available to them in the new system of competition once their old means of employment have disappeared. This may be a little clearer if one turns again to Engels' final draft: 'Principles of Communism'. Part of his answer to Question 10 (In what way do proletarians differ from manufacturing workers?) is as follows: 'The manufacturing worker is torn out of his patriarchalrelation by big industry, loses whatever property he still has, and in this way becomes a proletarian'.[45] Part of his answer to Question 11 (What were the immediate consequences of the industrial revolution and of the division of society into bourgeoisie and proletariat?) is that by means of the industrial revolution the power of the old classes is replaced by that of the bourgeoisie.[46] So, turning back to the *Manifesto*, the 'fight' is constituted merely by the very act of taking part in the technically free competition of the new system dominated by the bourgeoisie. The proletarians were thus enhancing the power of the bourgeoisie while diminishing that of the once powerful classes. Once again Marx was thus employing a metaphor to portray a process more dramatically.

Marx went on to describe the way in which the proletariat develops to the point at which it does begin to fight for itself; but this time the fight is against the bourgeoisie that has brought it into being. This happens because, as it increases in size and concentration, the proletariat gains in strength. The growing use of machinery meant that the distinctions in the interests and conditions of members of the proletariat were disappearing and the deskilling that this involved reduced wages to similar rates at low levels. These wages were, moreover, determined by the need of each member of the bourgeoisie to maintain profit and continue to build capital in the competitive environment that brought about periodic commercial crises. As the conditions of the proletariat became increasingly harsh the struggles between, on the one hand, individual workers within this class and, on the other hand, their particular bourgeois employers were becoming in each case so similar in nature that the many struggles were being transformed into broader collisions between classes. The growing recognition by the proletarians that they needed to unite with one another to keep wages at tolerable levels had led them to form combinations or, in other words, trades unions. This was in order to prepare for the revolts that occasionally broke out, sometimes taking the form of riots. Although this only achieved at most short-lived gains, in the longer term the union of workers was expanding. Very importantly, the rapidly improving means of communication and transport enabled different groups of workers to contact one another.

The rise of the proletariat to such a position was eased to some degree by divisions among the bourgeoisie of which, as mentioned earlier, Marx was fully aware. As the proletariat gained in unity and strength they had sometimes been able to exploit those divisions within the capitalist class. The point he stressed at this stage in the *Manifesto* was that although the proletarians were continually thwarted in their struggle because of divisions among themselves, they were nevertheless still achieving incremental gains because of bourgeois disunity. 'Thus', he suggested as an example, 'the ten-hours' bill in England was carried' (p. 82).

Marx's emphasis on the British Ten Hours Act, passed by parliament in 1847 to restrict the working hours of women and children, indicates of course that this was a gain that had registered in his mind as being of great significance. Indeed, in his later work he considered the results of this bill as a platform that could be built upon in order to achieve further gains by means of parliamentary legislation, even in a society that was fundamentally capitalist.[47] While revolution would still be required for a full transition to a communist society, he would stress in the later work, parliamentary activity should be undertaken in order to wring whatever concessions could be gained in the meantime and to start the process leading to the eventual transformation.[48] He wrote the *Manifesto*, however, from the point of view that revolution was likely to succeed very soon in the present phase of the epoch of the bourgeoisie (a view that would soon fade after 1848). At this time, while not discounting the value of parliamentary politics to the communist cause, he saw the bill in the main as a sign of the imminent demise of the bourgeois economy and state.[49]

The bourgeoisie was, as Marx perceived the situation in 1847–48, contributing still further to its own decline by calling on the proletariat to participate in the struggle whereby the power of the earlier dominant classes would be broken. The metaphorical fight mentioned above thus becomes relevant again at this point. The proletariat were enrolled in the struggle through their labour for the bourgeoisie, rather than for the older classes. By coming together into larger working groups, the proletarians were beginning to experience the unity in numbers that would eventually enable them to mobilize against the bourgeoisie. The political and general education that would thus be gained would prove to be very valuable to the proletariat. As Marx put it in the *Manifesto*, the bourgeoisie itself thus 'furnishes the proletariat with weapons for fighting the bourgeoisie' (p. 82). This can be seen in structural terms as the early stages of consolidation of units in industry, resulting in cooperative forms of work which helped people to develop the capacity to organize politically. As will be seen later in this guide, in the preface to the German edition of the *Manifesto* in 1872 Engels and he would suggest that this capacity had become far more advanced in the years since the pamphlet had first been published.

At this point in the *Manifesto* Marx's narrative undertook another change, albeit a rather subtle one. Having rather surreptitiously moved from discussing what had already taken place to anticipation, it now began more transparently to interpret what was happening even as he wrote. The ruling class had begun to disintegrate as sections within it found themselves unable to continue with the competition. Among these sections some people were falling into the proletariat. The ranks of the proletariat thus gained some new and valuable recruits (p. 82). Others, meanwhile, were coming to see that the threat of such a change in their social position was growing ever nearer.

Marx then switched once again to a position from which, while as before portraying the struggle as one of history, he was in fact looking forward to events that, he expected, would bring the epoch of the bourgeoisie to a close. 'Finally', he wrote in this vein, 'in times when the class struggle nears the decisive hour' (p. 82) (the decisive hour being the point in the process at which the ruling class and indeed the old society itself would collapse), a small section of that class changes sides to join the revolutionary proletariat. This section of the bourgeoisie, he stressed, would include 'a portion of the bourgeois ideologists, who have raised themselves to the level of comprehending theoretically the historical movement as a whole' (p. 82).

Marx's comment about bourgeois ideologists requires a little attention to his conception of ideology if one is to grasp his point firmly. This is because his conception is narrower and thus rather different to one that is widely held today – the latter perceiving an ideology as a body of political ideas and some view, plan or programme with regard to action by means of which to change or conserve society accordingly. For Marx, an ideology was a body of ideas that was idealistic and apologetic. It was idealistic in that the people who held this body of ideas assumed consciousness to be detached from the concrete world in which humans live. Consciousness was assumed to be the property of spirit which transcended the natural and social world. Marx viewed Western philosophy, including the recent Hegelian schools, to have been dominated by such a view of consciousness which very generally permeated thought in society. Indeed, his and Engels' book *The German Ideology* to which a number of references have already been made in this guide, was critical of such a philosophical tradition. Ideological thought regarded abstract ideas as possessing their own autonomous nature, thus overlooking the reality of the situation which was that general ideas are human products that conceptualize particular experiences and social relations. Idealists considered the ideas and experiences of their own classes to be natural and in turn believed their own values and interests to be universally valid. They thus became apologists for their own classes or groups.[50]

Marx often used the term 'ideology' to refer to the body of ideas that is biased in this way towards the dominant class in a society or legitimates that class; but as will be seen later in this chapter, such a body of ideas biased towards a class other than the dominant one could also qualify as an ideology.[51] Marx was nevertheless hoping that, just as he and Engels had from their middle-class upbringings rejected ideology and chosen to provide intellectual guidance to the proletariat in their struggle, others would take the same journey.

Marx went on in the *Manifesto* to stress the difference between the proletariat and all other classes. The proletariat was the only one that was genuinely revolutionary. Except for those among them who aligned themselves with the proletariat, members of other non-bourgeois classes wanted to 'roll back the wheel of history' (p. 83). This was because, following the dominance of the bourgeoisie, these other classes faced ruin and were thus conservative or reactionary. Those, furthermore, whom he referred to in the original German as *lumpenproletariat* – which is traditionally translated inaccurately as the 'dangerous class' or 'social scum' (p. 83) – would be more likely to be tempted by incentives to help prop up bourgeois dominance than to attempt to bring it down in a revolution. This class comprised the poor, uneducated masses: people who were unable to fully comprehend either the situation itself or ways to change it. They could be dangerous to the dominant class if not given such incentives. In fact, in the 1840s, the proletariat itself was considered to be a mass of thieves and paupers leading lives of misery. These people would be in this class for various reasons but, significantly, unlikely to be found capable of working in modern industry. These were not, however, the sort of people whom Marx considered as proletarians. Although those who comprised Marx's proletariat were in poverty, their poverty was a result of the artificial circumstances of capitalism. This revolutionary class was indeed capable of leading a revolution and then running modern industry and society. By describing this class as the proletariat Marx was using the word in a rather dissimilar way to what had been the norm during that decade.[52]

Like the class that had hitherto been commonly recognizable as the proletariat, Marx's proletarians according to him held no property in this late and dangerous hour of the epoch of the bourgeoisie. Members of the proletariat did not feel anything in common with bourgeois life and they no longer felt any allegiance to the nation. 'Law, morality, religion' had come to seem in the eyes of the proletarians to be 'so many bourgeois prejudices behind which lurk in ambush just as many bourgeois interests' (p. 83). Nevertheless, as mentioned above, members of Marx's proletariat were capable of participating in revolution. These proletarians would not, however, be able to follow the pattern whereby previous classes that were able to rise to challenge for the control of society had subjected that society to new conditions of appropriation. This was because the society to be introduced by the proletariat would need to abolish private property. Otherwise the new society would be just another example in the history of systems of appropriation.

Unlike previous transfers of power from one dominant class to the next, the proletarian revolution would, furthermore, be the work of a movement of the vast majority. It would, consciously, be in the interests of that majority. To emphasize the immensity of the fundamental change that would be needed to introduce the new and better society Marx went on to make another of his dramatic comments. In the Moore translation, rather than serve the purpose of illustrating, this comment unfortunately in fact merely obscures the point he was trying to make. The proletariat could not stir and rise itself up, he claimed, 'without the whole superincumbent strata of official society being sprung into the air' (p. 83). Carver's translation is clearer: 'without flinging into the air the whole superstructure of social strata which form the establishment'.[53] This translation also, incidentally, helps substantiate Marx's statement in 1859 that the *Manifesto* was one of the works through which his guiding thread ran. As was mentioned earlier in this guide, he would outline the guiding thread that year in the 'Preface to *A Critique of Political Economy*'. He said in that piece that the whole superstructure of society with its legal, political and other sectors would need to be overthrown. In other words, the superstructure that served the interests of the fundamentally bourgeois economic structure of society would need to be abolished in order for the transformation to be expedited.

Although, as will be seen later in this guide, he considered that the class struggle would ultimately be an international one, Marx conceded that the proletariat must first win their struggles at the respective national levels. It would, as he put it in the *Manifesto*, be necessary for the proletariat of each country 'first of all to settle matters with its own bourgeoisie' (p. 83). Basically, the point was that while he expected proletarians of the world to unite, it would be a mistake for them to wait for a simultaneous worldwide revolution. This would not happen. Revolution needed to target the actual structures and organizations that underpinned the dominance of the bourgeoisie because it was by such means that international capital was in turn represented and defended. The detail and significance of this feature of the *Manifesto* will become more evident towards the end of the study in this guide of the main text of the pamphlet.

At this point the first section of the *Manifesto* begins to draw to a close. First, however, in a short but quite crucial paragraph, Marx recaps in different terms one of the key narratives of the pamphlet discussed thus far: that of the development of the proletariat through several general phases. Once again portraying this process in terms of historical events he envisaged in the later stages a 'more or less veiled civil war, raging within existing society, up to the point where that war breaks out into open revolution' (p. 83). Significantly, the word 'sway' in the Moore translation that had featured in his discussion of bourgeois power comes into play at this point too. 'Sway' had, as will be recalled, been used to refer to the control by means of overwhelming economic and political power that the bourgeoisie had achieved in the modern epoch. Now, according to Marx, the revolution would lay 'the foundation for the sway of the proletariat' (p. 83). Such sway would not, however, be achieved in the manner that previous rising classes had experienced. Society had always been characterized by the antagonism of oppressed and oppressing classes. The epoch of the bourgeoisie had been similar in this respect but the new society would, by way of contrast, not be characterized by class antagonism.

Furthermore, the approach to the forthcoming era of sway would differ from that of previous periods insofar as, in those earlier cases, the classes that would in the future dominate had been able to improve their position in the period before they achieved sway. For example, the bourgeoisie had risen as industry had progressed, becoming so powerful that it became the new oppressing class as one epoch gave way to the next. This was not, however, something that the proletariat was experiencing. The modern labourer was, rather, sinking to the level of pauper. The proletariat was thus experiencing a worsening condition of impoverishment rather than improvement. The revolution would need to abolish the existing system of property rather than achieve the completion of a system that had already begun to develop (pp. 83–84). The experience to which the proletariat was being subjected would, Marx stressed, thus have profound, world-changing implications.

In the course of his discussion of the contrast between the forthcoming transition, on the one hand, and previous transitions, on the other hand, Marx quite suddenly offered a different angle from which to view the developments that were leading to the revolution. The bourgeoisie would no longer be fit to be the ruling class of society. This would be because the bourgeoisie would no longer be able to secure the existence of those it exploited. The crucial point Marx is making here is that the bourgeoisie in its relationship with the worker 'has to feed him, instead of being fed by him' (p. 84). He did not elaborate on this point but one can see more clearly what he meant by recalling that the bourgeoisie can exist only by exploiting the workers. If competition reaches the stage where it has driven wages so low that the workers can no longer sustain themselves to the extent that they can work, capitalism will no longer be able to operate. If the bourgeoisie would have to feed the workers then it would suffer a net loss rather than a net gain in the form of surplus labour which is, of course, the basis of its capital. The existence of the bourgeoisie itself thus, according to Marx, becomes 'no longer compatible with society' (p. 84). Society would no longer be able to live under that class that had been hitherto dominant. This is because once it could no longer engage in exploitation, the bourgeoisie would have lost the ability to exist *qua* bourgeoisie and thus, of course, would no longer be able to hold sway.

Meanwhile industry continued to have the potential to advance, even though the bourgeoisie was unable to make use of it. This advance of industry had though, as was discussed earlier, enabled the previously isolated labourers to associate and combine in ways which would make them genuinely revolutionary. Marx had by now reached the point where he was ready to present two important sentences with which to summarize and conclude the first section of the *Manifesto*. 'The development of Modern Industry', he suggested, 'cuts from under its feet the very foundations on which the bourgeoisie produces and appropriates products' (p. 84). While he did not mention productive forces at this point (to do so would probably have spoilt the effect) one can see that this was in fact what he had in mind. Those forces were becoming too advanced for the existing mode of production because they could create an abundance of goods. Workers who became aware would hence no longer tolerate exploitation and poverty. They would expect a decent standard of life. The material conception of history is thus significant here. The next sentence, which is one of the most memorable of the entire pamphlet, served to emphasize that the fall of the bourgeoisie and the rise of the proletariat would be part of one process. What the bourgeoisie produced, this sentence exclaimed, were 'its own gravediggers' (p. 84). This is a metaphor so graphic that it probably needs no explanation. Nevertheless, the point he was making has been summarized very well by Jules Townshend, who suggests that, for Marx, 'capitalism had an in-built tendency to self-destruct and create the necessary conditions for a classless society'.[54] Workers who would no longer tolerate capitalism would, if one might extend the metaphor, consign the system that exploited them to the grave.

Study questions

1 How did Marx summarize the history of all society?
2 In the series of epochs through which history progressed what did Marx suggest was different about the one he was experiencing?

3 What is the significance of contradiction in the argument presented in the first main section of the *Manifesto*?

4 When reading the *Manifesto* why is it useful to consider what Marx had in his earlier work discussed in terms of alienation?

5 As the proletariat approached the point at which it would achieve sway, how, according to Marx, did the proletariat differ from previous classes in such situations?

6 What did Marx mean when he said that the bourgeoisie become their own gravediggers?

7 What were the key points of Marx's conception of ideology?

'Proletarians and communists'

As was discussed in the previous section, in his 'Theses on Feuerbach' of 1845 Marx had proclaimed that though the philosophers had interpreted the world in various ways, the task now was to change it. While in the first main section of the *Manifesto* he had offered his own interpretation of the world, in the second section he began to fulfil the task that he had set himself in the 'Theses'. In other words, he was concerned with steps that might be taken to begin to bring about the appropriate changes to the world. Having anticipated the consignment of capitalism to its grave, he turned his attention at this point to the replacement of the bourgeois economic structure. This would in turn bring about the replacement of what he would later, as we have seen, refer to as the superstructure that had been built upon it. This structure and superstructure would, he hoped and expected, be forced by means of revolutionary action to give way to a new, non-exploitative arrangement. Accordingly, in the second section, Marx offered a brief sketch of the sorts of measure that would be needed to bring about the transition to communism.

Marx's first task in this second section was to clarify the role of the communists, who would lead the revolution, and their relationship with the proletariat. The reason for beginning the section in this way might not be immediately apparent. One approach he might have taken would have been to move swiftly on from the demise of the bourgeoisie to the features of the new epoch that would take its place. The motive for taking a different course comes into view, however, once one recalls the fundamental purpose of the *Manifesto*. Although many of its themes were discussed at length in the other works of philosophy or political economy by Marx, or by Marx and Engels together, the *Manifesto* was essentially a political pamphlet and, indeed, what it was declared to be: a manifesto. As such one of its key purposes was to deal with transition, rather than to present a vision of the ideal society. As will be seen later in this guide, he criticized some of his rivals and earlier socialists for presenting such utopian visions.

As a pamphlet, moreover, the *Manifesto* was presenting the standpoint of the Communist League. As was discussed earlier in this guide, the League was an organization that had been given the designation of 'Communist' as late as 1847. It almost immediately came to be influenced profoundly by Marx and Engels. Marx was concerned in the *Manifesto* not only to criticize the opposition, to present strategy and tactics, and to outline the future goal of communism to which such tactics and strategy were intended to lead. He was also presenting the partisan case to his readers that the League was the appropriate organization to follow in order to pursue that goal.

Having opened the section by posing the question of the relation between the communists and the proletarians as a whole, Marx announced that the communists did 'not form a separate party opposed to other working-class parties' (p. 84). The interests of the communists were not, moreover, 'separate and apart from those of the proletariat as a whole' (p. 84). They did not have their own sectarian principles 'by which to shape and mould the proletarian movement' (p. 84). The communists could, however, be distinguished from other parties of the working class in that during the national struggles the latter parties tended to distinguish between nationalities. Sharing the interests of the international proletariat as a whole, the communists represented and campaigned for the common interests of that entire class. This approach was, he stressed, maintained throughout all the stages of the conflict with the bourgeoisie.

To grasp fully why Marx was seeking to appeal to such a wide audience one needs to recall once again that he and Engels, while residing in Brussels, were drafting and writing the *Manifesto* at the request of other leaders of the London-based League which, in its new form, sought to attract broad support rather than act as a conspiratorial sect. Fundamentally, moreover, the movement would, eventually, need to be international in order to introduce a sustainable communist society.

In its old guise as the League of the Just, the organization had come into existence in 1837, in Paris. For much of the 1840s the League had, in this earlier form, found it necessary to compete with rival radical organizations, some of which had been formed as a result of splits in the League itself. The members of the League in London were looking to reunite the different factions. Marx and Engels were given considerable freedom regarding what to include in the *Manifesto*. This was in order to keep them on board and to encourage them to produce a document that would appeal to many of the groups which, they hoped, would be interested in forming a new international organization.[55]

The change of name to the Communist League was part of the reconstitution from an organization mainly interested in revolutionary conspiracy to one of open propaganda, aiming to attract wider support from proletarians.[56] In the period covering the reorganization, the renaming of the organization and the publication of the *Manifesto* Marx's influence on the programme and policy of the League grew. Its statutes began to announce as its main purposes the overthrow of the bourgeoisie and the ending of class society and private property.[57] These are, of course, purposes that are at the heart of the *Manifesto*. This helps shed light on why, in the early paragraphs of the second section, Marx commented that the communists did not form an organization separate from the various parties and did not have sectarian interests that were made on behalf of the League. In the hope of reuniting the radical factions, readers of the *Manifesto* were being told indirectly that they could trust the Communist League to be an organization which would have no such interests.

After he had in the first few sentences of the section distinguished the communists from other parties, Marx went on to promote the League very directly. He declared that the communists were the most resolute of all the working-class parties of each country. The communists, he insisted, had a clear understanding of 'the line of march, the conditions, and the ultimate general results of the proletarian movement' (p. 85). The communists thus had a theoretical advantage over the rest of the movement. They pushed all other working-class parties forward.

As this was a campaigning pamphlet Marx did not elaborate on the line of march in the sort of theoretical terms he would later use in some of his other works. At this point the *Manifesto* may, indeed, be rather frustrating to readers who approach his work from a perspective of political philosophy. Let us therefore investigate.

Two points here are particularly significant. First, Marx's emphasis on the theoretical advantage of understanding the way forward, the conditions and the results can be seen in terms of the guiding thread that, he would later suggest, had been a feature in the *Manifesto*. As we have seen, this thread applied the dialectical method to the study of the history of society. The theory was, he insisted, not based on the ideas or principles of any general reformer. It was rather based on the observation of what was actually happening in the world (p. 85). By drawing on his guiding thread one can see that what was in fact happening was, for Marx, the latest stage in the dialectical process in which forms of property relations were being abolished and subsequently replaced with new ones that had been immanent within them. An earlier example of such stages and transition between them was the abolition of feudal property and replacement by the present bourgeois property which was actuated by means of the French Revolution. The forthcoming transition would, he stressed in the *Manifesto*, be very different. As the property to be abolished was bourgeois private property, this would be 'the final and most complete expression of the system of producing and appropriating products, that is based on class antagonisms, on the exploitation of the many by the few' (p. 85).

The second of the two significant points concerning theoretical advantage over other working class parties is as follows. As has just been mentioned, the communists did not seek to work independently of other like-minded parties but rather to work with them in a leading role. Marx did not name any such parties at this stage in the *Manifesto*. He did so very briefly, as will be discussed later in this guide, at the beginning of Section Four of the pamphlet. The immediate aim of the communists in working with all these parties was to form the proletariat into a class, to bring an end to bourgeois supremacy, and to lead the proletariat to political power.

As has already been discussed at several places in this guide, the fundamental purpose of seizing power would be to bring about a society in which private property itself would be abolished. This would of course be a policy that would attract opposition from those who were served by the old order. The purpose of the latter order was equally as fundamental as that of the revolutionaries. As one would probably expect, Marx anticipated criticism from the defenders of the free market on this point. The communists, those defenders had alleged, sought to abolish the personal right of people to acquire as property that which was the fruit of their labour. The personal freedom, activity and independence of individuals, moreover, depended, according to these critics, upon the defence of that right.

In his response to such allegations Marx took the opportunity that this presented to clarify the position that both he and the League had formulated on private property and the abolition thereof. In the present epoch the development of industry was already bringing destruction to the property of artisans, peasants and other classes whenever so doing served the interests of the bourgeoisie. Modern bourgeois private property, furthermore, was not the fruit of bourgeois labour. It was, rather, based on the exploitation of wage labour. The capital that was thus accumulated by the bourgeoisie was, moreover, a social product, relying on the effort not principally of individual members of the bourgeoisie but on all the members of society. Hence, when capital would come to be converted into common property by means of the forthcoming revolution, the result would not be conversion of personal property into social property. Property had in fact always been social but its character had been determined by the class relations of each mode of production. It would be this class character that would be lost (p. 86).

Although a key purpose of the *Manifesto* was to contribute to and help further the political struggle in practice, Marx was thus also making a hugely important contribution to political philosophy with regard to the notion of property rights. This is something that may be missed because this mention of property in terms of rights was only brief. What was crucial in his response was the suggestion that arguments which considered property rights to be acquired on the basis of the supposedly hard work of individuals were in fact unsound because of a false premise. The property was actually gained by taking the fruits of the labour of many individuals whose work together created social products. To get a tighter grasp on this important feature of the *Manifesto* it is useful to refer briefly to one of Marx's earlier compositions that have already been mentioned in this guide: 'On the Jewish Question'.

In 'On the Jewish Question' Marx had treated the idea of civil or human rights with disdain. These were the rights that had become known as the rights of man since the French Revolution. The notion of such rights was, however, grounded on what, for Marx, was a fundamentally mistaken conception of human beings as simply selfish and egoistic creatures by nature. Nevertheless, because of the perceived division between the public and the private that had come to be the received wisdom in capitalist society, people did see themselves as private individuals. Citizenship was subsequently interpreted according to individualism, and the common good was understood in such terms. Individuals operating in this mindset did not associate with one another as though they were members of communities. They became in effect atomistic individuals and were thereby separated from their essentially social nature.[58]

Marx was thus concerned that those advantages that were widely perceived in the epoch of the bourgeoisie as property rights were in fact based on the taking of socially created produce without due recompense. This brings back into the picture the exploitation that, as we have seen, was in Marx's view involved in wage labour. With this in mind, he suggested in the *Manifesto* that the wage which was deemed the minimum necessary to pay the workers was determined in terms of the means of subsistence or, in other words, in terms of that which was absolutely necessary for the continuing existence of the labourer (p. 86). Marx said that this was the average price of wage labour. Hence, the labourer appropriated from their work just enough for a bare existence to be prolonged and reproduced. This was a practice that Marx was resolute to change, and so this brings us to another of the key themes of the *Manifesto*: the issue of what sort of society would be built after the proletarian revolution. Even here, Marx was concerned to discuss practical measures rather than offer a utopian vision of the future.

In one of the first hints in the *Manifesto* of what he hoped to achieve after the abolition of the capitalist mode of production, Marx stressed that he and his fellow communists by no means intended to abolish personal appropriation of the means to life and its reproduction. What they did intend to change were the circumstances of such appropriation. People would no longer have as their primary role the accumulation of capital for the benefit of their exploiters. The opportunity to appropriate enough even for mere subsistence would, furthermore, no longer be at the discretion of a ruling class. The communist society would thus be very different from the capitalist one it was intended to replace. Accumulated labour would be 'but a means to widen, to enrich, to promote the existence of the labourer' (p. 86).

In the bourgeois society, Marx continued, living labour was used merely as a means to increase accumulated labour. Living persons had lost their individuality and had become dependent on others. Capital, meanwhile, had become independent and enjoyed a sense of individuality. What he was suggesting in a rather obscure way can be brought into the spotlight if one considers once again the views on alienation that he had expressed 4 years before the publication of the *Manifesto*. People suffered from this condition of alienation when the creative origins of things they had produced from nature were not acknowledged. Such people became dominated by those products as personal worth was interpreted in terms of exchange value. The object that labour produces, he had suggested in 'The Economic and Philosophical Manuscripts' of 1844, 'confronts it as an alien being, as a power independent of the producer'.[59]

This process of alienation was, in Marx's view, a feature of the continuing operation of the capitalist mode of production with its system of wage labour and exploitation. This should be borne in mind as the narrative of the *Manifesto* continues with Marx's suggestion that defenders of this mode complained that to abolish it would be to thereby abolish individuality and freedom. The individuality and freedom that the bourgeoisie enjoyed in the capitalist mode, he responded, resulted in this lack of individuality and freedom for the many, and so it was right to abolish bourgeois individuality, independence and freedom.

In fact, Marx went on in the *Manifesto*, the buying, selling and free trade upon which bourgeois freedom depended would be abolished along with the bourgeois conditions of production and the bourgeoisie itself. Anticipating expressions of horror from the defenders of private property, Marx offered as a riposte the following observation: 'But in your existing society, private property is already done away with for nine-tenths of the population; its existence for the few is solely due to its non-existence in the hands of those nine-tenths' (p. 87). After declaring that the bourgeois commentators were in fact correct in their view that the communists wanted to do away with their property, he struck again from another angle. The bourgeois position was, he thus suggested, that individuality would vanish once labour could no longer be converted into capital. This was in fact bourgeois capital, which was in effect a social power that the majority faced. The implication of this position was, he stressed, that the term 'individual' applied only to the middle-class owners of property. This was a social role that would be abolished and indeed 'made impossible' (p. 87) by the new communist system.

The notion of being made impossible is very significant. Marx's point was that the person *qua* bourgeois owner of property would not be able to emerge from the communist social system. To be that sort of person a human being had to become one of the minority whose activity prevented the other nine-tenths from accumulating what they needed for a decent standard of life. Communism would not allow this to happen. 'Communism', indeed, he insisted, 'deprives no man of the power to appropriate the products of society; all that it does is to deprive him of the power to subjugate the labour of others by means of such appropriations' (p. 87).

Marx went on to respond to another objection to communism that its opponents had been voicing. This was that no work at all will be done in society once private property has been abolished. The society to come, it was alleged, would in such circumstances be one of universal laziness. 'According to this', he retorted, 'bourgeois society should long ago have gone to the dogs through sheer idleness; for those of its members who work, acquire nothing, and those who acquire anything do not work' (p. 87). This way of responding to the objection may appear a little odd. It becomes clearer if one recognizes that Marx was constructing an argument of the sort that philosophers refer to as a counter-example. The counter-example in this case served two purposes. First, it helped rebut an important challenge regarding the viability of communism. Second, it helped support his allegations of exploitation in capitalist society very clearly.

In this case his counter-example was constructed as a riposte to the argument that people would not work in a society where private property had to be abolished. He was for this purpose stressing that the very existence of capitalist society depended upon many people having no choice but to work for little or no more than the means to sustenance while a minority did not work. This, he was thus suggesting, helped refute the proposition that people would not work if there were to be no private property. His argument was that in today's society many though not all people work, but none of the many gains significant private property. This meant that they were exploited. The minority did not work but did amass private property by exploiting the majority that did work. That particular situation would be reversed in the new society.

Let us look at the workings of this counter-example a little more closely. The argument that Marx was opposing was, as we have just seen, that in communist society, where private property would be abolished, no work would be done. The weakness of this argument is countered by Marx's example which helped him allege that private property had been in effect abolished for 95 per cent of people. Yet those people did work because they had to labour for a wage, which was in turn because of the social power wielded by the bourgeoisie.

Although the counter-example does hit its target it is not one of Marx's more lucid ones. His argument was on far stronger ground at the point where he suggested that the whole of this objection, like all others against the communist method of appropriation of material, intellectual and cultural products, was actually 'an expression of the tautology that there can no longer be any wage labour when there is no longer any capital' (p. 87). What he was implying here was that while wage labour would indeed disappear, it would be incorrect to say on the basis of this tautology that there will no longer be any production at all.

Similarly, the narrative of the *Manifesto* continues, it was incorrect to say that if the culture associated with classes were to disappear there would be no culture remaining at all. What would be lost would be the particular culture in which the vast majority of people were expected to act almost like machines which maintain the wage labour system. Marx was arguing for the introduction of communism which, he contended, would not deprive people of the power to appropriate. Important here is the point that having the power to appropriate but not to exploit others in order to do so implies having actually to work in order to so appropriate.

This is because power is in this context the ability to do something, and work is the application of that ability for some purpose. They would not be deprived of such power to gain a decent standard of living. Furthermore, the culture that helped sustain the system in which it was considered acceptable for people to be exploited would disappear.

The exposure of generalizations that were employed by critics of communism continued in the *Manifesto* as Marx reproached from another angle those who attempted to vilify communist intentions to abolish bourgeois property. To this end he condemned such critics for applying their own bourgeois notions, such as those of freedom and law, as though they were derived from eternal laws of nature or reason. He identified inconsistency on this point. On the one hand, they were correct to portray as mistaken the ideas of the classes which were dominant before the era of the bourgeois society. On the other hand, on the basis of a 'selfish misconception' (p. 88), they presented bourgeois ideas as though they were laws of nature or reason. They did not realize that just as the ideas of previous dominant classes sprang from the existing mode of production and types of property of the era, their own ideas were rooted firmly in the conditions of the bourgeois production and property. The character and direction of laws were determined by the conditions on which the bourgeoisie depended for the continuation of its existence (p. 88).

Marx's attack on the bourgeoisie for portraying their ideas as universal was in fact something more than criticism of this particular point; once again he was using the dialectic method. As was discussed earlier in this guide, his method involved a materialist variant of the dialectic. The point about the ideas and laws being rooted in and determined by production, property and conditions reflects this materialist approach. The ideas of pre-bourgeois dominant classes reflected the material conditions of their times. As the development of productive forces had rendered those ideas outdated, the portrayal of them in universal terms was shown to be mistaken. The introduction of the bourgeois mode of production had resolved the earlier contradiction between forces and relations of production. Conditions, however, had changed. As the productive forces now promised to expose the inaccuracy of the present assumption of the universality of ideas, this new contradiction would itself need to be resolved by moving on from the bourgeois mode of production. This can all be seen to fit more neatly into the broader purpose of the *Manifesto* if one takes another brief look at Marx's 'Preface to *A Critique of Political Economy*' which, in 1859, identified the pamphlet as an earlier piece through which the guiding thread of his studies had been sewn. 'At a certain stage of their development', Marx insisted in the 1859 preface, 'the material productive forces of society come into conflict with the existing relations of production'. The relations of production, which had once constituted forms of development of those productive forces, had reached, or at least were approaching the stage at which they become transformed into their fetters. 'Then', he stressed, 'begins an epoch of social revolution'.[60]

Having briefly criticized the erroneous assumptions of universality regarding bourgeois ideas and laws, Marx appears at this stage in the *Manifesto* to change course quite abruptly as he mentions the communist proposal for the abolition of the family. Even the most radical thinkers, he announced, 'flare up at this proposal' (p. 88). The way in which this statement bears continuity with the discussion it followed is not at all obvious. This, however, is another place at which, if one follows the narrative carefully, the coherence of the pamphlet may become more evident. His point about the family fits once more into what, as discussed in Chapter two of this guide, Engels would later call the materialist conception of history.

Marx stressed that even this institution of the family was dominated by the requirements of the existing mode of production. His account emphasized the hypocrisy of bourgeois attempts to conceal the actual situation of families during the epoch of the bourgeoisie. The present form of family, he insisted, was developed in the bourgeois epoch and based on capital and private gain. Even the wives of bourgeois men were considered by the latter as no more than instruments of production (pp. 88–9). It is useful to consult Engels' second draft – 'Principles of Communism' – again at this point in order to achieve greater clarification of this criticism. In his answer to Question 21 of the catechism he stated that the two bases of traditional marriage that communism would abolish were those of 'the dependence rooted in private property of the woman on the man, and of the children on their parents'.[61]

The high morality preached by the bourgeoisie was, according to Marx, 'clap-trap' (p. 89). It was even more objectionable because it masked the reality of exploitation that permeated the bourgeois approach to both their own families and those of the proletariat. Bourgeois men considered their wives as mere instruments; some of these men, furthermore, seduced the wives of their fellow bourgeoisie. Bourgeois marriage was, behind the moralistic veneer, in effect 'a system of wives in common' (p. 89). Turning to the wives and daughters of the proletarians, he stressed that their economic position rendered them vulnerable to abuse. All this, along with the use of prostitutes by bourgeois men, was in effect the reality of the community of women which the bourgeoisie accused the communists of wishing to introduce but which, on the contrary, communism would abolish.

In the new communist society, according to Marx, the present bourgeois family would disappear, as would what was in fact the absence in practice of the family among proletarians. What he meant by this becomes clearer with his statement that in bourgeois society 'all the family ties among the proletarians are torn asunder, and their children transformed into simple articles of commerce and instruments of labour' (p. 89). The dominant class was thus in control of an economic system of which a feature was child labour. Neither this nor public prostitution would any longer exist.

Continuing his concern about the experiences of children in capitalist society, another aspect of family life with which Marx was concerned was that of their education. He noted that communists had been criticized for wanting to replace education at home with social education. Education in bourgeois society was, he responded to this charge, also social, albeit in a different way. Education was determined by the social conditions of the day, and these conditions required such education to be dominated by the influence of the ideas of the ruling class. Communism would indeed introduce a new social form of education when the old bourgeois-dominated form vanishes along with the bourgeois family itself and the violations of proletarian family life.

Having thus dealt with the bourgeois criticism of communist views on the family, Marx returned to a point he had mentioned very briefly at the start of this second main section of the *Manifesto*. This was the issue of nationality. The communists were not tied to particular countries but, nevertheless, still had to organize at national levels. He reiterated this point in anticipation of criticism on the grounds that the communists would abolish countries and nationality. In support of his position on this issue he suggested that differences and antagonism between peoples were vanishing rapidly. Of course, this prediction has turned out to be only partly correct. While some differences can be seen to have diminished as a result of the cosmopolitan nature of capitalism, the history of warfare since he wrote these words makes the rapid vanishing of antagonism a far less accurate forecast.

This point about nationality, like that of the family, was linked to the general themes of the *Manifesto* and other works by Marx that incorporated the guiding thread of his studies. Nationality was waning, he suggested in the *Manifesto*, 'owing to the development of the bourgeoisie, to freedom of commerce, to the world market, to uniformity in the mode of production and in the conditions of life corresponding thereto' (pp. 89–90). As the proletariat gained supremacy, he went on, the differences and antagonism would diminish still more quickly. This would happen because the proletariat would need to unite in order to prepare the conditions for the emancipation of their class.

Looking back from the standpoint of the twenty-first century one has to acknowledge that such unity that he predicted in the mid-nineteenth century has not yet transpired. There is, moreover, no way of knowing whether the vanishing of antagonism would have taken place in other circumstances. Marx's confidence that this would happen is testament to his faith in what would later be described as the materialist conception of history, the features of which, as we have seen, he and Engels had started to present in some of their earlier works.

This materialist conception becomes still more evident as the narrative in the second main section of the *Manifesto* moves on. Consciousness, which included the ideas and views of man, was subject to change, he suggested, 'with every change in the conditions of his material existence, in his social relations and in his social life' (p. 90). As material production was changed, so was the character of intellectual production. This meant that in each age the ruling ideas had been those of the ruling class. The materialist nature of the dialectic that Marx considered to be at work in the epoch of the bourgeoisie is perhaps at its clearest at this point in the pamphlet, where he considered what was really happening when people mentioned the ideas that revolutionize society. The very significant fact that such people were expressing was 'that within the old society the elements of a new one have been created, and that the dissolution of the old ideas keeps even pace with the dissolution of the old conditions of existence' (p. 90).

This notion of elements of a new society being created within the old one is often described today in terms of immanence. The critical nature of Marxism has, moreover, sometimes in the twentieth and twenty-first centuries been portrayed as immanent critique. For Terry Eagleton, for example: 'Marxism as a discourse emerges when it is both possible and necessary for it to do so, as the "immanent critique" of capitalism, and so as a product of the very epoch it desires to move beyond.'[62] While there is no need at all for readers of the *Manifesto* to study the Critical Theory tradition in which this notion of immanent critique is often found, it is useful to note, however, that such critique involves analysis whereby contradictions are found in society between, on the one hand, practices and their justifications and, on the other hand, possible alternatives that involve solutions to the problems that those practices bring, and which their justifications conceal. This notion of immanence is thus useful to the understanding of the materialist conception of history. This can be appreciated further by referring again to Marx's 'Preface to *A Critique of Political Economy*', in which, as we saw earlier, he described a 'legal and political superstructure' that is built on the economic structure consisting of the relations of production that bring about class conflict. In a comment in that preface which indicates that, as was mentioned earlier in this guide, Marx did not conceive of ideology as necessarily a body of ideas biased towards the dominant class, he said that at the level of the superstructure there are 'ideological forms in which men become conscious of this conflict and fight it out'.[63]

Ideology thus featured on each side of the class struggle. What is interesting here is that Marx believed the proletarian point of view to be limited and partial just like any other ideology. While he of course sympathized with the view of the proletarians, he was under no illusion that he was one of them. He believed that intellectuals like himself, Engels and others in the Communist League needed to lead the proletarian revolution and offer guidance for the building of the new society. Such guidance would not be ideological as it was neither idealist nor apologetic.[64] As we have seen, he insisted that the 'productive forces developing in the womb of bourgeois society' created 'the material conditions for the solution of that antagonism'.[65] This metaphor of the womb illustrates clearly the notion of immanence which in turn helps one grasp where, according to Marx, the important developments in productive forces actually come from. Those developments, furthermore, needed to be fettered in order for the bourgeois mode of production to be sustained. The ideological forms of consciousness of the dominant class contributed to this fettering. The inconsistency between, on the one hand, the capabilities of the productive forces and, on the other hand, the impression of such capabilities as portrayed by the powerful ideological resources of the dominant class needed to be resolved.

To return to the *Manifesto*, Marx's point about the dissolution of old ideas is followed by three paragraphs in which he discussed the process whereby, through the ages, ancient religions had given way to Christianity, which in turn gave way to the rational ideas of the eighteenth century. As the revolutionary bourgeoisie had brought about the demise of feudal society, the ideas of religious liberty and freedom of conscience reflected the sway of free competition. Of course, critics of communism were not wrong to stress the continuity that had always characterized capitalist society. While certain religious, moral, philosophical and juridical ideas had been replaced by others, religion, morality, philosophy, political science and law more generally indeed continued to exist. Communism, it was alleged by such critics, would by way of contrast abolish all religion, all morality and all eternal truths. Unlike the previous changes whereby religions and morality were modified in accordance with historical development, communism would put an end to these institutions in their entirety.

Marx was ready to respond to such criticism. He offered the riposte that what this accusation reduced itself to was a response to the following reality: 'The history of all past society has consisted in the development of class antagonisms, antagonisms that assumed different forms at different epochs' (p. 90). All the previous ages shared the characteristic of exploitation of one part of society by another part. It was, hence, for Marx hardly surprising that the social consciousness, which was dominant in each of those ages, took similar forms and accommodated ideas general to them all. In the process of moving on from the exploitation that was a feature of all those earlier ages those general ideas would vanish completely;

this would require class antagonisms to disappear from society entirely. Communism would be necessary to bring about such fundamental social change. 'The Communist revolution', Marx insisted, 'is the most radical rupture with traditional property relations; no wonder that its development involves the most radical rupture with traditional ideas' (p. 91).

Marx at this point declared that he had finished responding to bourgeois objections to the fundamental social and political changes that communism would entail. He now began to consider in more detail just what the communists would need to do in order to bring about the necessary radical changes to society. In a sentence crucial to the entire *Manifesto* he declared that 'the first step in the revolution by the working class is to raise the proletariat to the position of the ruling class, to win the battle of democracy' (p. 91).

To gain a fuller understanding of Marx's ideas on political and social change it is useful to focus for a moment on his reference, in the sentence just quoted, to both revolution and democracy. Some people may consider the mention of the two concepts in the same sentence rather strange. Indeed, as Eagleton has recently discussed, revolution and democracy are often considered to be the opposites of one another. This, however, is to misunderstand the concepts and their use by Marx, Engels and Marxists after them. Only ultra-leftists (or, in other words, people who refuse to have any dealings whatsoever with the existing state) dismiss entirely the need for and value of parliamentary democracy and social reform. Many Marxists, including Marx and Engels themselves, have advocated the use of parliamentary democracy and social reform, but with the expectation that at some point the system will refuse to give way any further. This is the point at which vested interests can no longer give concessions. The parliamentary democracy that can be accommodated in the capitalist order allows opponents of the dominant class to do no more than work in a system of which, ultimately, they have no control. Bearing in mind that the essence of democracy is fundamentally about control by the people, parliamentary democracy is simply not democratic enough for Marxists who recognize its value.[66]

With this clarification in mind one can appreciate that democracy was thus indeed a key concern for Marx. Looking back at the declaration that winning the battle of democracy was the first step we might recall that, as was discussed earlier, Marx had always shown great interest in the Ten Hours Act as an example of how advantage may be taken of divisions among the bourgeoisie. Marx believed that, at least in some countries such as England, Holland and the United States, the communists and their allies may be able to gain control of the political system by constitutional means.

Further clarification of Marx's point about the place and function of democracy in the process can be gleaned from Engels' second draft. Here one finds in clear terms the basis for Marx's far more stylistic yet rather less unambiguous comment about the battle of democracy. In his answer to Question 18 of 'Principles of Communism' (What will be the course of this revolution?) Engels suggested that the revolution would 'establish a democratic constitution, and through this, the direct or indirect dominance of the proletariat'. Democracy, he argued nevertheless, 'would be wholly valueless to the proletariat if it were not immediately used as a means for putting through measures directed against private property and ensuring the livelihood of the proletariat'.[67] Putting through such measures would be the point at which the vested interests would need to be challenged, thus going far beyond the first step.

That to actually go beyond the first step would, in Marx's view, require considerable organization, speed and commitment on the part of the revolutionaries is clear from the remainder of this section of the *Manifesto*. The proletariat would, upon winning the battle of democracy, 'use its political supremacy to wrest, by degrees, all capital from the bourgeoisie, to centralise all instruments of production in the hands of the State . . .' (p. 91). This new state would take the form of 'the proletariat organised as the ruling class' (p. 91). Hence, the political sway, or control, mentioned earlier would have passed from the bourgeoisie to the proletariat, who would need to 'increase the total productive forces as rapidly as possible' (p. 91).

In stressing the need to press forward quickly with the fundamental changes to society, Engels and Marx were acutely aware of the possibility of forceful reaction on behalf of the vested interests of that society. They expressed this awareness in different ways. Before looking at Marx's view in the *Manifesto* of how to move forward in this environment, we will get a fuller picture by turning first to Engels' emphasis on the gravity of the problem in very similar passages in each of his two drafts. These passages can be found in his answers to Question 14 of the first draft, which asks whether the Communists reject revolution, and Question 16 of the second draft, which asks whether the peaceful abolition of private property will be possible. In each case he stressed how useless and harmful conspiracies can be. He emphasized that communists would certainly take a peaceful path to the abolition of property if the opportunity were to arise. The structural element of the materialist approach was clear in these passages, where he reasoned that revolutions were not made intentionally or arbitrarily but were brought about by conditions that were dependent on the will and direction of neither individuals nor classes. What nevertheless had been very clear to the communists was that throughout its development in most countries which he referred to as 'civilized', the proletarian class had been violently suppressed. 'If', he warned in the second draft (there being, significantly, an almost identical sentence in the first) 'the oppressed proletariat is finally driven to revolution, then we communists will defend the interests of the proletariat with deeds as we now defend them with words'.[68]

When Marx received the second draft he transformed it to emphasize the solution rather than the problem. Hence, it is useful to bear Engels' comments in mind when one reads what Marx had to say on the matter. At the start of the process this would, according to Marx, need to involve 'despotic inroads on the rights of property, and on the conditions of bourgeois production' (p. 91). Such inroads would, he stressed, 'appear economically insufficient and untenable . . .' (p. 91). The measures the inroads introduced would nevertheless go on beyond themselves. He seems to have been suggesting that their value would become apparent later. The measures would need to be followed by 'further inroads upon the old social order' (p. 91). Importantly, these despotic inroads were 'unavoidable as a means of entirely revolutionising the mode of production' (p. 91). He was not at all clear why there would need to be further such inroads. Bearing in mind Engels' concerns, however, it would appear that Marx expected unrest and a refusal of opponents of the revolution to cooperate, bringing about an economic crisis that would necessitate further measures to consolidate the revolutionary changes.

On the one hand, Marx's revision of Engels' draft resulted in a relative lack of clarity regarding the situation to be tackled.

What, on the other hand, was gained was the replacement of what readers might have seen as a slightly hesitant approach on the part of Engels with Marx's more confident tone that did not shy away from the nature and extent of the struggle that lay ahead. Winning the battle of democracy as the first step would need to be followed by despotic inroads; but unless rapid progress were to follow, thus making these inroads a temporary phenomenon followed by further progress, then the revolution would be likely to fail.

Marx said that the measures he described as despotic inroads would differ from country to country but listed ten which could be considered applicable fairly generally. All ten of these measures were radical in the circumstances of their time. While some still retain their radical appearance today, however, others seem rather mild, especially in countries that have enjoyed substantial periods of government on the basis of a welfare state, often set up by social democratic or labour parties in power, but maintained even under liberal or conservative governments. Although in times of economic crisis the gains brought about by the welfare state sometimes come under pressure from vested interests of capitalism, the reversal of some measures that have been achieved since Marx advocated them would be controversial to say the least. The reintroduction of others after having in some countries been reversed would not be considered particularly revolutionary today.

Among the ten measures those which seem most mild by the standards of many but by no means all parts of the world today were the second, the first part of the seventh and the first two parts of the tenth. The second was: 'A heavy progressive or graduated income tax' (p. 91). The first part of the seventh was: 'Extension of factories and instruments of production owned by the state' (p. 91). The first two parts of the tenth would to many people today seem the least radical of all. These were: 'Free education for all children in public schools. Abolition of children's factory labour in its present form' (p. 92).

Turning to some of the other measures, we can with hindsight see that the implementation of the fifth would, like the mild ones just mentioned, be possible without the need for capitalism to be transcended. This fifth measure was: 'Centralisation of credit in the hands of the state, by means of a national bank with State capital and an exclusive monopoly' (p. 91). This had, indeed, been advocated earlier by Pierre-Joseph Proudhon as a measure that could be introduced in a capitalist society.[69] This is interesting as Proudhon was, as will be discussed in the next section of this guide, one of the thinkers of the Left whom Marx criticized later in the *Manifesto*. Nevertheless, these relatively mild measures, when combined with the others in the list, together make for a radical communist programme that was designed to strike at the heart of the capitalist system.

Of the other, more radical measures in the list of ten, the fourth, which assumed that there would be considerable opposition from the vested interests, was: 'Confiscation of the property of all emigrants and rebels' (p. 91). This measure serves to indicate that Marx expected such fervent dissatisfaction with the revolution in some quarters as to spark a significant departure by the opponents of the new society. These emigrants would, according to the measure, have to leave their property behind and thus be unable to contribute to the impoverishment of the country in transition. The measure also serves as another indication that Marx expected some form of rebellion from the society's counter-revolutionaries, whose assets would hence be seized.

The extent of the despotic inroads that Marx deemed necessary upon victory in the battle of democracy is also illustrated by Measure One on the list: 'Abolition of property in land and application of all rents of land to public purposes' (p. 91). The progressive nature of the revolution – in other words, the contribution to public or social purposes – is, furthermore, announced in this measure. Being the first measure in the list it was a sensible tactic on the part of Marx to flag to his readers this reason for the implementation of the measure. The second part of Measure Seven seems also to have been conceived with the contribution to social purposes in mind. This was 'the bringing into cultivation of waste-lands, and the improvement of the soil generally in accordance with a common plan' (p. 91).

The third measure was: 'Abolition of all rights of inheritance' (p. 91). This was perhaps the measure most likely to lead to the emigration of the wealthy who would, one would expect, attempt to take their assets. This was a problem for which Marx sought to prepare by means of Measure One. Turning to the sixth measure, which may seem very mild in comparison with the first, it called for: 'Centralisation of the means of communication and transport into the hands of the State' (p. 91). Many states that introduced extensive welfare systems in the second half of the twentieth century also implemented significant nationalization processes including transport and communications. The potential extent of nationalization of transport, however, made this measure particularly radical in Marx's time. It was the combination of this with the others in the list that contributed to a programme that would, as Marx expected, make a counter-revolutionary challenge a distinct possibility.

The eighth measure in Marx's list was: 'Equal liability of all to work. Establishment of industrial armies, especially for agriculture' (p. 92). The first part of this measure may not seem particularly alarming to vested interests. It is the second part – that of massive state intervention with industrial/agricultural armies – which would be likely to be worrying to those interests. Once again, however, the real impact would be felt in combination with the rest of the measures. This is also the case with the ninth: 'Combination of agriculture with manufacturing industries; gradual abolition of the distinction between town and country by a more equitable distribution of the populace over the country' (p. 92). These ten measures together illustrate the extent of change that Marx hoped for in the early stages of development of the post-capitalist society. He hoped, however, that this would be just the start of a far more extensive transformation.

Marx hoped that his ten measures would eventually lead to a society in which there would be no place for class distinctions. Having no useful purpose, such distinctions would subsequently disappear. In the process the whole nation would work as an association and the public power would have lost its political character. 'Political power, properly so called, is', he elaborated, 'merely the organised power of one class for oppressing another' (p. 92). To reach the point where the political character of public power could disappear the proletariat would have, as he had discussed earlier in the *Manifesto*, to organize itself as a class. It would have been compelled to do so because of the force of circumstances whereby exploitation would have worsened to make life intolerable. By means of revolution the proletariat would, having become an organized and ultimately ruling class, sweep away the conditions which had brought about classes in the first place and the antagonisms between them. The role of the proletariat as a ruling class would thus be only temporary, as by ridding society of the class antagonisms it would abolish its own class supremacy – it would no longer, indeed, be a class properly defined at all. 'In place of the old bourgeois society with its classes and class antagonisms', he declared in conclusion to this section of the pamphlet, 'we shall have an association, in which the free development of each is the condition for the free development of all' (p. 92).

This well-known statement about free development gives an indication that Marx was not the advocate of crude, austere egalitarianism. Had he been so, this may indeed have warranted portrayal in terms of a spectre or horror story, such as he had introduced sardonically in the preamble to the pamphlet. As Eagleton has stressed, Marx was not 'opposed to individualism', and indeed did not wish to sink the individual 'in some faceless collective'. His aim, Eagleton continued, was a very different one: 'to re-establish communal bonds between men and women at the level of their fully developed individual powers'.[70] Human nature was thus indeed malleable, in that, free from the suppression of exploitative dominant classes, humans would be able to develop as fully as the nature of the species could accommodate.[71]

Marx, Engels and their communist colleagues were thus appealing for support for their campaign for a new society in which humans could enjoy natural development. Having presented his own case Marx, as was mentioned earlier in this guide, criticized a range of other socialist and communist thinkers and groups who/which had already voiced their ideas. These included earlier communists who did advocate austerity and crude egalitarianism.

This brings us to another key theme of the *Manifesto*: the variants of socialism and communism. As will be discussed in the next section of this guide, Marx and Engels considered it necessary to devote a significant part of the pamphlet to their criticism not only of the early communists but also of a variety of groups which could be located within a broadly defined socialist tradition that had begun to emerge since the French Revolution of 1789.

Study questions

1 Why was Marx so concerned at the beginning of Section 2 of the *Manifesto* to clarify the nature and purpose of the Communist League?

2 On what grounds did Marx criticize the influential notion of property rights?

3 Why did Marx describe the high morality preached by the bourgeoisie as 'clap-trap'?

4 What did Marx mean when he said that the proletariat could win the battle of democracy?

5 Why did Marx consider winning the battle of democracy to be merely the first step?

6 Given that some of Marx's ten measures to be implemented when the proletariat gained power were relatively moderate, why should the measures be considered radical when grouped together in a programme?

7 Why is the concept of immanence so helpful to the understanding of Marx's argument?

'Socialist and communist literature'

By the time Engels and Marx respectively drafted and wrote the *Manifesto* just under 60 years after the French Revolution had broken out in 1789, the bourgeoisie had reached a dominant position in some countries. In other countries this rising class was at various stages towards dominance. For Marx, this rise of the bourgeoisie was a necessary stage in the development of the productive forces. When they came to be further developed, those forces would require the demise of the capitalist class that had fostered and nurtured them in this bourgeois epoch. Marx, as has been discussed in this guide, was convinced that the demise would require class struggle. There were others who sought alternatives to capitalism without seeing the need for such struggle. Some were early communists but many others were known as socialists. These communists and socialists were mutually unsympathetic to one another. France was particularly well represented in this broad category comprising variants of what we would now call the Left.

As Thomas has commented and as will be discussed in this section on Marx's criticism of socialist and communist literature, the French prominence in the socialist movement sheds light on

Marx's rather curious inclusion at the beginning of the *Manifesto* of French radicals among the opponents of communism.[72] Marx, it may be recalled, mentioned such radicals in this context in the very first paragraph, where he listed anti-communist individuals and groups who/which had entered into alliance as a means to attempt to exorcise the spectre of communism.

While the term 'French radicals' may thus apply to some of the socialist groupings that Marx criticized in the pamphlet, other groupings were backward looking, and thus were far from being radical. Marx agreed that early steps had been taken in the campaign to introduce some sort of socialism. Nevertheless, as the *Manifesto* as a whole makes very clear, he considered that much still needed to be done, as any attempt to achieve a real socialist society would face determined opposition from the vested interests of the existing order. In his criticism of the different contributions to this socialist tradition Marx divided the various groups and thinkers into three broad categories that were progressively less backward looking. The first of these categories was reactionary socialism; the second was conservative or bourgeois socialism; the third was critical-utopian socialism or communism. He divided the reactionary socialist category into three groupings: feudal socialism; petty-bourgeois socialism and German or 'true' socialism.

The first of Marx's attacks in the *Manifesto* on reactionary socialism – his assault on feudal socialism – centres on a discussion of aristocratic criticism of the bourgeoisie for the latter class's leading role in undermining traditional social and economic arrangements. 'Owing to their historical position', Marx stated, 'it became the vocation of the aristocracies of France and England to write pamphlets against modern bourgeois society' (p. 92). This mention of a 'historical position' is significant. Marx's approach, as has been mentioned a number of times already in this guide, was one which Engels later summarized as the materialist conception of history. In the feudal mode of production the aristocracy had occupied a dominant position. Now that the bourgeoisie had acquired economic and political sway, however, the position of the aristocracy had changed – it had lost its role as the dominant class in society.

Even when this point about the historical role of the aristocracy has been placed in the context of Marx's broader approach in the *Manifesto* (an approach that, as we have seen, is found indeed in much of his other work) an understandable reaction might be to ask what this has to do with socialism at all. An answer can be found in one of the many informative footnotes that Frederic L. Bender has added to his edition of the *Manifesto*. As Bender suggests, Marx used the term 'socialist' in a pejorative sense to describe all sorts of reformist literature.[73] This included the literature of the anti-bourgeois aristocracy.

Indeed, as Thomas suggests, by the time that Marx and Engels presented the case for communism, the socialist movement had been growing for a number of years in ways that helped distinguish it from communism. In the *Manifesto* Marx criticized early communism as well as the socialist movements and doctrines which craved respectability. Marx considered socialism, as opposed to communism, to be such a moderate approach as to be able to accommodate within itself the aristocratic criticism of capitalism. Communism, for him, would involve no such accommodation. This view reflected the common understanding of socialism and communism in the early to mid-nineteenth century. As McLellan puts it in his Introduction to a recent edition of the *Manifesto*, 'whereas "socialism" tended to be a rather pacific term associated with utopian schemes, "communism" was a more militant word, which connoted the abolition of private property'.[74] While militant early communism was in Marx's view too austere, he nevertheless sought to establish the new communism as an autonomous and predominantly proletarian movement.[75]

Although, as was mentioned earlier, he was not opposed to alliances, Marx believed nevertheless that the autonomy of the modern communists should still be maintained to a significant degree. When he wrote the *Manifesto* he perceived socialism as a weak doctrine and, moreover, saw it as a movement which grasped neither the problems of society nor the necessity for a revolutionary solution. The feudal socialism of the aristocrats was particularly poor in this respect, warranting a scathing attack rather than any alliance.

The feudal socialists, Marx argued, resorted to literature alone, neglecting the need for action. Their position as a defeated class ruled out a serious political struggle on the basis of the ideas they published in their pamphlets. The French Revolution of July 1830 replaced the monarchy which, since being reintroduced in 1814, had defended the aristocracy. In its place was put another monarchy, but this time one that favoured the bourgeoisie. Furthermore, the English reform agitation had helped bring the Reform Act of 1832 which extended the franchise to more of the wealthy property owners. These events in France and England had further consolidated the position of the bourgeoisie. Hence, the literature of feudal socialism had achieved very little in the way of real impact (p. 92). The aristocrats resorted to lamenting the old order and lampooning or, in other words, ridiculing, the bourgeoisie. Although the aristocrats were desperately trying to claw back power, this effort was dressed up as genuine concern for the working class. The latter class had, nevertheless, seen through this desperate attempt. Feudal socialism was, Marx taunted in another comment that illustrates his recognition of modernity, 'always ludicrous in its effect, through total incapacity to comprehend the march of modern history' (p. 93).

Marx hinted very briefly at the sorts of writers who, in his view, belonged to this feudal socialist category. They included a section of the French legitimists and the thinkers of the Young England movement. The former were those who, in the attempt to win legitimacy for the restoration of the Bourbon monarchy, criticized the hardships that bourgeois rule had imposed upon the working class. The Young England movement comprised conservatives such as Carlyle, the future Lord Shaftsbury and Disraeli.[76] Marx's own lampooning of this English group may seem rather wide of the mark given the literacy success of Carlyle and Disraeli, and the eventual political success of Disraeli who later in the century served as prime minister. Indeed, Marx himself would occasionally express respect and appreciation for Disraeli's political skills. Given, however, that Disraeli's attempts to ally the aristocracy and working class against the bourgeoisie were intended to conserve rather than radically transform the existing condition of society, Marx's cutting analysis in the *Manifesto* was perhaps more astute than may at first seem to be the case.[77] Marx saw the need for progress rather than reaction with its limited gains for the working class.

The feudalists, Marx noted, insisted that the exploitation which had taken place during the period of dominance of their own class was not at all like that of the bourgeoisie. This, Marx reminded readers, was simply because their own circumstances and conditions were different from those which had since emerged. Their own had now become antiquated. This, incidentally, was yet another indirect reference to the approach that came to be known as the materialist conception of history. Changes in the material circumstances and conditions ensured that the organization of society had changed accordingly. The modern proletariat had, indeed, not existed under the rule of the aristocracy; but the feudal socialists needed to be reminded of the crucial point that 'the modern bourgeoisie is the necessary offspring of their own form of society' (p. 93). The bourgeoisie was bound to bring into existence a class that would eventually destroy the old society. It had indeed done so and that class was the proletariat (the bourgeoisie had thus – one might suggest, borrowing one of the analogies Marx had used earlier in the pamphlet – created their own gravediggers). The aristocrats, while speaking on behalf of the proletariat with the motive of achieving stability and harmony, were actually worried about the potentially revolutionary nature of that exploited class. In political practice the aristocrats did not refrain from either imposing coercive measures against the working class or engaging in practices detrimental to that class when this was deemed necessary.

All the points in Marx's account of feudal socialism are quite straightforward once one is accustomed to, first, his approach, second, his fundamental theory and, third, his style of writing. This account is followed, however, by the following rather obscure, single-paragraph sentence: 'As the parson has ever gone hand in hand with the landlord, so has Clerical Socialism with Feudal Socialism' (p. 94). What this meant was that religion had often been employed to help maintain the economic position of the dominant class.

Marx argued that Christianity was similarly being used in the present epoch, but this time it was in the service of the previously dominant but now declining aristocratic class. Christian asceticism was being given a 'Socialist tinge' (p. 94). This, he implied, had little real effect on society. 'Has not Christianity', he asked, 'declaimed against private property, against marriage, against the state?' (p. 94). Clearly this had produced little impact. 'Has it not, he went on to ask, 'preached in the place of these, charity and poverty, celibacy and mortification of the flesh, monastic life and Mother Church?' (p. 94). Such asceticism did nothing to improve the lives of the working class. 'Christian Socialism', he suggested, in the final sentence of this division of the sub-section on reactionary socialism, was 'but the holy water with which the priest consecrates the heart-burnings of the aristocrat' (p. 94). Christian socialism, in other words, had merely provided solace to aristocrats who were ashamed of the exploitation they had once exerted.

Marx stressed that the feudal aristocracy was not alone as a class the power of which had been undermined by the success of the bourgeoisie. He had earlier in the *Manifesto*, one may recall, discussed some other such classes and the ways in which their power was undermined as the bourgeoisie consolidated its power. Some of the classes were actually precursors of the bourgeoisie such as the medieval burgesses and small peasant proprietors. In the societies that were in the lower stages of capitalist development, the power of these old classes had not been diminished entirely. Rather, the burgesses and small peasant proprietors 'still vegetate side by side with the rising bourgeoisie' (p. 94). The materialist conception of history is in evidence yet again here. In this case, however, what Marx said about older classes vegetating implies that the dialectical process assumed by the materialist conception will often be a very slow and gradual one.

A class which Marx considered worthy of special focus was the petty bourgeoisie. The literature offered by this class could, he suggested, be seen in terms of petty-bourgeois socialism – his second division of reactionary socialism. This is another point in the *Manifesto* at which a rather strange designation becomes clearer if one remembers that he used the word 'socialist' pejoratively to describe reformist literature in general. This petty-bourgeois class fluctuated between the proletariat and bourgeoisie in countries where modern civilization had become fully developed. It was 'ever renewing itself as a supplementary part of the bourgeoisie' (p. 94). He illustrated the fluctuation he had just mentioned by noting that the competition by which the present society was characterized served to hurl down individual members of the petty bourgeoisie into the proletariat. Eventually, with the development of modern industry, the disappearance of the independent petty bourgeoisie in the sectors of manufacturing, agriculture and commerce altogether had begun to loom. The members of the class would be replaced in these sectors by overlookers, bailiffs and shopmen.

Marx turned his attention briefly to the situation of the peasantry in France. As far more than half the populace of the country were peasants it was, he suggested, understandable that criticism of the bourgeoisie, by writers who sympathized with and spoke for the proletariat, would be voiced in terms that reflected the experiences of the peasantry and petty bourgeoisie. Marx nevertheless stressed the weakness of such petty-bourgeois socialist criticism. 'Sismondi', he suggested, 'was the head of this school, not only in France but also in England' (p. 94). To get a clearer picture of the point that Marx was attempting to convey it will be useful to consider the views he expressed elsewhere in his works on the theories of Jean Charles Simonde de Sismondi.

At this point it is useful to note that when one refers to the work of a thinker with the aim of corroborating or clarifying a point he/she had made earlier, it is important to proceed with care because of the possibility that his/her view may have changed over time. We should adopt such caution as we consider Marx's discussion of Sismondi in *Theories of Surplus Value*, which was written in the 1860s (but which remained unpublished in Marx's lifetime). Now although this guide will not look in detail at the prefaces of the later editions of the *Manifesto* until the end of this chapter, an exception is made here. This is because, several years after Marx wrote *Theories of Surplus Value*, the preface that he and Engels wrote for the German edition of the *Manifesto* of 1872 included a sentence of great significance. 'However much that state of things may have altered', they wrote with reference to the conditions of 1848, 'the general principles laid down in the *Manifesto* are, on the whole, as correct today as ever' (p. 103). Those general principles of course were largely those of the materialist, historical understanding of any particular point in time. The economy and society developed in conjunction with the growth of productive forces. Politics and other elements of the superstructure developed accordingly. We can, therefore, assume that Marx considered the general principles of the *Manifesto* to still be correct when he wrote about Sismondi in *Theories of Surplus Value*, a few years before Engels and himself wrote the 1872 preface.

One of the section headings in Chapter 19 of *Theories of Surplus Value* is as follows: 'The Unhistorical Outlook of Classical Economy'. Here one finds criticism of Sismondi which helps readers to make sense of Marx's very brief mention of him in the context of socialism in the *Manifesto*. In that particular section of *Theories of Surplus Value* Marx gave Sismondi credit for being 'profoundly conscious of the contradictions in capitalist production'.[78] One of the assumptions at the heart of Marx's thought was, it may be recalled, that material contradictions emerged when one condition made another untenable because of the nature of the relation between them.[79] One such contradiction was that which tended to develop between the continuation of a mode of production and the development of productive forces. Sismondi, he suggested, knew that production relations which stimulated unrestrained development of productive forces and wealth, were conditional. Their 'contradictions of use-value and exchange value, commodity and money, purchase and sale, production and consumption, capital and wage-labour, etc.', Marx suggested, 'assumed greater dimensions as productive power develops'.[80] There was, furthermore, he went on, a fundamental contradiction of which Sismondi was particularly aware; this was that the unrestricted development of productive forces and increase of wealth were in contradiction with the restriction of the mass of producers to the necessities of life. Sismondi perceived crises, Marx continued, as essential, large-scale outbreaks of the immanent contradictions at definite periods.

Though he did thus recognize that part of Sismondi's analysis was correct, Marx's far more critical categorization of the latter thinker in the *Manifesto* as a reactionary socialist becomes clearer when one reads further into the passage in *Theories of Surplus Value*. Knowing that the contradiction would need to be resolved one way or another he wavered, Marx suggested, between, on the one hand, the view that the state should curb productive forces and, on the other hand, the recommendation that relations of production be made adequate to the productive forces. Hence, Sismondi, retreating into and eulogizing the past or criticizing without fully understanding, sought (and here Marx found another opportunity to use the terminology of the supernatural) to exorcise those contradictions by means of adjustments and redistribution. Sismondi did so without realizing that the scope was very limited for such action given that he was unwilling to contemplate transcending the existing relations of production. He did not understand that there were processes whereby the contradictions could actually be resolved.[81]

This brief look at some of Marx's later views on Sismondi helps throw light on the statement in the *Manifesto* that the petty-bourgeois school of socialism 'dissected with great acuteness the contradictions in the conditions of modern production' (p. 94).

This school had presented incontrovertible proof of the disastrous effects that machinery and the division of labour were having upon the working class because of the harsh inequalities in the distribution of wealth. It saw very well not only that the proletariat endured misery in the existing conditions of anarchy in production but also that the peasantry and the petty bourgeoisie themselves faced ruin. The school recognized, moreover, that the vast scale of modern warfare between nations was also a result of the present system, as were the dissolution of the old moral bonds, family relationships and nationalities.

While Marx thus gave credit to petty-bourgeois socialists for understanding the problem, he believed them to be hopelessly weak regarding the solution to it. They considered such a solution to involve either one of two forms, both of which Marx considered to be reactionary. First was the restoration of the old means of production and exchange along with their corresponding property relations. The second form of the solution involved the containment of the bourgeois means of production and exchange within their old framework of property relations. That framework was already waning following the development of productive forces and would eventually be exploded. This older framework would involve 'corporate guilds for manufacture; patriarchal relations in agriculture' (p. 95). The distinction between these two considerations for solution is quite subtle. In the first case there would be a full restoration, while in the second case there would be containment of much of the present economic arrangement within the old framework. To believe either of these two forms of solution to be possible was, he insisted, reactionary and, using a word that he would apply to another category of socialism more directly, 'Utopian' (p. 95). 'Ultimately', he said in summary of his dismissal of this petty-bourgeois school, 'when stubborn historical facts had dispersed all intoxicating effects of self-deception, this form of Socialism ended in a miserable fit of the blues' (p. 95). Perhaps more effective is Carver's translation of the original source of the sentence just quoted: 'In its later development this tendency petered out in a pusillanimous hangover.'[82]

Turning to the third division within his reactionary socialist category, Marx noted that the socialist and communist literature which had first begun to emerge in France had later been introduced into Germany. This literature formed the basis of what he called

German or 'True' Socialism (p. 95). This adoption and adaptation of the French ideas took place in the 1840s – a time when the struggle of the bourgeoisie in Germany was at a far less advanced stage than had been the case in France. Indeed, the struggle in Germany was only just beginning. This meant that the imported ideas lacked practical significance as the conditions in which they had originally been expressed in France were very different from those of the country to which they were now being applied. Those ideas were hence interpreted in general terms of practical reason. Having originated as 'utterances of the will of the revolutionary French bourgeoisie', they had signified to the German philosophers of the late eighteenth century 'the laws of pure Will, of Will as it was bound to be, of true human Will generally' (p. 95). The German literati had indeed merely annexed the ideas as they might translate directly from a foreign language, without bearing in mind that their own philosophical tradition was likely thus to distort the message of those ideas.

A problem that readers may find at this point in the *Manifesto* is that Marx's critical discussion of the true socialists in the pamphlet is not particularly illustrative of its target. Hence, in order to glean a clear picture of the context of his criticism it is useful first to bear in mind some general comments that he and Engels had made a few years earlier in the section titled 'True Socialism' at the beginning of Volume II of *The German Ideology*. Noting that it was these German socialists who had styled themselves as true socialists, Marx and Engels criticized them for absorbing English and French communist ideas into their own thoughts while failing to regard those ideas as the expression and product of an actual movement. The problem that resulted from this negligence, Marx and Engels reasoned, was that these true socialists regarded the ideas they had adopted as purely theoretical writings which had evolved as pure thought. The true socialists could not grasp that the foreign ideas from which they drew inspiration sprang from the practical needs and conditions of life of a particular class in its own country. Unable to examine the real state of affairs or to understand the context of the ideas, the true socialists attempted in vain to clarify those ideas. The problem that led to the confusion on the part of these so-called socialists stemmed from their perception of those ideas as having connections to the German philosophical tradition to which Hegel and Feuerbach belonged.[83]

It is useful to recall at this point that (as was mentioned earlier in this guide) Marx had abandoned the ideas of Feuerbach and the other Young Hegelians very early in the development of his thought. A footnote that Engels added to the *Manifesto* in 1890 is significant in this respect. He mentioned in that note, which he placed at the end of the discussion of true socialism, that 'the chief representative and classical type of this tendency is Mr. Karl Gruen' (p. 97). Gruen, or Grün as his name is more often spelt, was one of the key contributors to the true socialist doctrine. Marx and Grün were engaged in intense rivalry in the 1840s, attacking each other in philosophical, political and personal terms.[84] Marx and Engels criticized Grün's belief that the true German version of socialism was superior to the French and his enthusiasm for the thought of Feuerbach, this being part of a broader eulogy to the German philosophy on which true socialism drew.[85] Given that Marx's political philosophy built on his earlier criticism of Feuerbach and Hegelianism it is hardly surprising to find true socialism as one of the doctrines included in those subjected to the *Manifesto*'s criticism of reactionary socialism.

Rather than focus upon real human beings, Marx and Engels had suggested in *The German Ideology*, the true socialists were concerned with the more abstract 'man'. Proclaiming the universal love of mankind, they had lost any revolutionary enthusiasm. As a result, they did not see the proletariat as the class that was capable of bringing about the necessary changes to society. Such a role the true socialists ascribed to the petty bourgeoisie and its philosophers, and thus to a sort of consciousness which was at that time influential in Germany.[86]

Returning to the *Manifesto* with these points from *The German Ideology* in mind, one thing that the reader will see quite clearly is that Marx did not hide his disdain for the universalistic German philosophy which, in his view, did not take into account historical and particular conditions. Marx indeed described as 'philosophical nonsense' the attempts to interpret the French ideas in the terms of the German philosophers. He compared such 'nonsense' to the 'silly lives of Catholic Saints' which the monks had written over 'classical works of ancient heathendom' (p. 95–6).

Marx offered examples of the German attempts to apply their universalism to French socialist criticism of the bourgeoisie. The first such example in the *Manifesto* was the attack upon the economic functions of money (or, in other words, monetary relations) which, according the true socialists, brought about the problem of 'Alienation of Humanity' (p. 96), or in the Carver translation 'externalisation of the human essence'.[87] The second was the true socialists' attack upon the bourgeois state by means of the claim to identify 'Dethronement of the Category of the General' (p. 96). Marx, or perhaps Moore as translator, was being rather vague here; but Bender offers some useful footnoted comments that help us begin to make sense of Marx's examples and, indeed, help clarify his criticism of true socialism. In the first case, as Bender reminds us, Marx and Engels were critical of the notion of the alienation of humanity because they were concerned to present their different concept of alienated labour in the endeavour to express the struggle between classes. As Bender suggests, this becomes evident as one reads on in the *Manifesto* after the vague examples mentioned above. Regarding the notion of 'Dethronement of the Category of the General', Bender notes that a more accurate translation would be 'abolition, transcendence, preservation of the rule of abstract Universality'. This is at least equally as vague. Marx's point, Bender suggests, was that the true socialists sought to 'go beyond' the liberal conception of society and the notion of equality of all citizens in the market and before the law, without taking into account other aspects of the social condition of such citizens.[88]

Bender's notes help illustrate Marx's rather vague suggestion that the true socialists intended to go beyond but not abandon generality. The picture becomes clearer still if one once again turns to Carver's translation, which replaces 'Dethronement of the Category of the General' with 'transformation of the reign of abstract generality'.[89] Why, the question arises, would he have said 'preservation' as well as 'abolition' and 'transcendence' as Bender suggests he does? What Marx seems to have meant was that the true socialists were being critical of the social condition of the bourgeois society and state, but were still attempting to resolve the problem by striving for actual equality and actual universality. They thus ignored the fact that the bourgeoisie had yet to reach the position of dominance in Germany. Such a position would need to be reached before the social conditions in that society could be addressed. The materialist conception of history is significant yet again here. The material conditions would have to develop sufficiently before the contradictions within them could be resolved.

The true socialists were, Marx went on, attempting to represent not true or actual requirements, but rather 'the requirements of Truth' (p. 96). In other words, as McLellan notes, they were attempting to turn French socialism into a metaphysical system.[90] Thus, for Marx, they did not get to grips with the need to overcome the fundamental class divisions that were essential features of the present and former epochs of modern history. German society was at such an early stage in the development of the bourgeoisie that the ideas which the true socialists were importing from France and interpreting in terms of German philosophy were irrelevant anyway. It was important to recognize that until capitalist society underwent significant development and until its class divisions were overcome through proletarian revolution, which would of course bring about the demise of the capitalist class, it would be futile to strive for genuine equality in any case.

Marx went on to suggest that both the fight of the bourgeoisie and the accompanying liberal movement against the older dominant classes in Germany were becoming more earnest. The true socialists were in effect presented with a great opportunity to confront the bourgeoisie and its allies with socialist demands. They were indeed able to attack the liberal tenets of representative government, bourgeois competition, bourgeois freedom of the press, bourgeois legislation, bourgeois liberty and bourgeois equality. They could preach to the masses that there was nothing to gain but everything to lose by supporting the bourgeoisie and its political movement. In attempting to emulate the French criticism of the bourgeoisie, however, the true socialists neglected the most important point. This was that the French 'presupposed the existence of modern bourgeois society, with its corresponding economic conditions of existence, and the political constitution adopted thereto' (p. 96). These tenets and conditions were in fact the things that, having yet to be achieved in Germany, were the objects of the pending struggle there.

To grasp the point that Marx was thus making, one needs to recognize that this was yet another place in the pamphlet at which the ideas that would later become known as the materialist conception of history were what he had in mind. The true socialists were criticizing tenets and conditions that needed to develop in the first place in order to leave the feudal mode of production fully behind. Only thus would the necessary conditions develop and become ripe for a proletarian revolution. The revolution would, in turn, use the productive forces that would, as he had mentioned earlier, otherwise continue to be held back by what would become the obsolete capitalist mode of production. All that the true socialists were actually achieving was the establishment of what the existing dominant class would consider 'a welcome scarecrow against the threatening bourgeoisie' (p. 96). This dominant class, which had suppressed the risings of the emerging German working class, was, he went on, actually being underpinned by the true socialists.

While it was the older dominant class that would thus have gained the most if the bourgeois society had been somehow undermined by the literature of the true socialists, the class that the latter thinkers were directly representing was that of the petty bourgeoisie. This lower middle class, to which Marx referred as the German philistines because of their unenlightened and unimaginative thought, had appeared and reappeared constantly and in various forms since the sixteenth century. The result of the representation of this class by means of the forestalling of industrial and political progress was the preservation of the old order which was wrapped in a transcendental robe – a 'robe of speculative cobwebs, embroidered with flowers of rhetoric, steeped in the dew of sickly sentiment' (p. 97). This 'robe' was thus a metaphorical one, which served to conceal the realities of power. By this means the true socialists were seeking to defend the existing condition of society from both the concentration of capital and the revolutionary proletariat. According to Marx they 'appeared to kill these two birds with one stone' (p. 97).

True socialism, according to Marx as he summarized his account of this doctrine, dominated the so-called socialist and communist literature available in Germany at the time when he and Engels were working on the *Manifesto*. Suggesting that the writers who belonged in this division of reactionary socialism considered the petty-bourgeois philistine to be the typical man within Germany which they saw as the model nation, he reminded readers that this was to neglect the fact that this was but a temporary situation that would be changed by progress. He said, moreover, that they interpreted this sort of man in a socialistic way that was 'the exact opposite of its real character' (p. 97). The true socialists opposed communism for being brutally destructive and held the communists' fundamental concern of class struggle in contempt. What Marx was suggesting in his dramatic prose was that the petty bourgeoisie which such socialists championed had in reality no interest in building an alternative to the bourgeois society – a society which 'true' socialism sought in vain to forestall. On this point the sub-section of the pamphlet on reactionary socialism, with its three divisions, was brought to a close.

The second broad type of socialism to which Marx extended his analysis in the *Manifesto* was the sort of thought he called conservative or bourgeois socialism (p. 97). Its aim was to redress social grievances in the interest of preserving the existing bourgeois society. As will become evident in a moment, one can find another comment that allows the significance of Marx's reference to French radicals at the beginning of the *Manifesto* to become somewhat clearer. This comes at the point in the narrative where he discusses a thinker whom he allocated to this category.

Into this conservative or bourgeois socialist category Marx placed a very broad and disparate range of groups. Somewhat disparagingly he listed those it covered as follows: 'economists, philanthropists, humanitarians, improvers of the condition of the working class, organisers of charity, members of societies for the prevention of cruelty to animals, temperance fanatics, hole-and-corner reformers of every imaginable kind' (p. 98). He suggested that complete systems had been devised on the basis of this form of socialism. What he meant becomes clearer as one reads on into the short sub-section on this category. Between that suggestion and the remaining paragraphs of the sub-section, however, Marx added, without elaboration or explanation, the following comment: 'We may cite Proudhon's *Philosophie de la Misère* [*The Philosophy of Poverty*] as an example of this form' (p. 98). Proudhon is widely recognized as an early, major thinker of the anarchist tradition. He was perhaps the thinker for whom Marx's label 'French radical' was most appropriate. Hence, this famous anarchist's inclusion into this conservative or bourgeois category may seem rather odd.

To understand why Marx cited Proudhon as an example of this sort of socialism, it is helpful to recognize that relations between these two leading thinkers of the nineteenth-century Left were characterized by intense antagonism. Marx's criticism of Proudhon was, moreover, part of his fundamentally hostile approach, both as a writer and as a political activist, to anarchism in general.

Like some other leading anarchists, such as Stirner and Michael Bakunin, Proudhon was in Marx's view overly concerned with and worried about the power of the state. The anarchists stressed the oppressive, authoritarian nature of the state and its determining influence in society. The anarchist revolution would, hence, be directed at the state. Marx was opposed to such an approach for two main reasons. First, throughout his writings he considered that the capitalist economy held primacy over the bourgeois state. He thus believed that, while they had identified one important target, the anarchists had neglected an even more difficult one on which revolutionaries would need to focus. Second, he opposed the anarchists for their outright opposition to authority. They were anti-authoritarian to an unrealistic and unnecessary degree.[91]

Marx's belief in the need for authority, albeit of a very different sort to that which had been experienced thus far in history, can thus be seen to be connected to his view of the role of political activity in the transition to a new society. He saw a need for class struggle to take place at the political level. The political struggle would help bring an end to the present economic mode of production. After the revolution a new form of authority would be needed – a form of authority suitable to the new basis for the communist society that would, gradually, be built. Hence, as was discussed earlier in this guide, he stressed in the *Manifesto* the need to win the battle of democracy.

In his writings Marx tended to distinguish between, on the one hand, power which was in his view, as was discussed earlier in this guide, wielded by the class that held the means to economic dominance, and, on the other hand, authority.[92] Proudhon's opposition to authority included not only a view of the necessity for change but also an approach which ruled out revolution led by a proletarian party. He opposed communism and had no conception of the sort of new society in which the productive forces could be advanced, and thereby production become more expansive.[93] Taking this into consideration, one can see why, in the *Manifesto*, Marx included Proudhon in the conservative or bourgeois category of thinkers who 'want all the advantages of modern social conditions without the struggles and dangers necessarily resulting therefrom'. Such thinkers, he went on, desired 'the existing state of society, minus its revolutionary and disintegrating elements' (p. 98). In other words, as Carver's translation states, they wanted that society without 'the revolutionary elements bent on destroying it'.[94] Marx was targeting Proudhon as such a thinker because of the latter's refusal to consider the need for the forward-looking sort of fundamental change that could be brought about by a revolutionary proletariat and the necessary authority it could put into operation. This helps one to appreciate Marx's comment that thinkers in this category would like to see a bourgeoisie without a proletariat. This type of socialist, he went on, develops 'into various more or less complete systems' (p. 98) the belief held by the bourgeoisie that its own world was supreme.

Marx was actually being a little unfair on Proudhon by categorizing him as such. Proudhon was, indeed, uncompromising in his own terms and did want fundamental social change. The problem that Marx perceived with this anarchist's thought was to do with the fact that it was founded on a belief that the abolition of the state would somehow allow ordinary people to prosper and enjoy fulfilling lives in their associations. Marx criticized those such as Proudhon who believed that changes in the material conditions of existence and in economic relations between people in society could be achieved by means of radical reform which would not involve political struggle between classes. A problem was that without such struggle such changes would necessarily have to take place within the framework of the existing relations of production. As Engels put it in his second draft ('Principles of Communism'), but without actually suggesting that Proudhon belonged in this category, what the bourgeois socialists wanted was 'to maintain this society while getting rid of the evils which are an inherent part of it'.[95] While Proudhon was more critical of the existing society than Marx's inclusion in this category seems to imply, Marx was, nevertheless, on firmer ground in his portrayal of him as a thinker who rejected the authority of any sort of political organization. Marx was not unreasonably questioning how the society might be changed without the guidance of some such authority. To fully comprehend Marx's rather mischievous criticism of Proudhon in this respect one should once again remember that the *Manifesto* was, as its title suggests, at least as much a political pamphlet as a piece of political philosophy. Focusing on Proudhon's rejection of the option of an organized proletarian campaign, Marx was able to promote his own revolutionary doctrine by distinguishing it from, and indeed portraying it more favourably than, that of one of the leading radicals of the early to mid-nineteenth century.

Marx finished his discussion of bourgeois socialism by listing a few of the things that such socialists sought to achieve. First there was free trade, but for the benefit of the working class. Then there were protective duties that were similarly presented as being for the benefit of the working class. Third was prison reform, once again intended to be in the interests of the working class. This variant of socialism was, he concluded, 'summed up in the phrase: the bourgeois is a bourgeois – for the benefit of the working class' (p. 98). As the whole of his first main section of the pamphlet illustrates, Marx was clearly of the view that any such benefits would be negligible and heavily outweighed by the treatment that in his view the proletariat was bound to endure in its role as the dominated class during the epoch of the bourgeoisie.

The third and final category of the socialist and communist literature with which Marx disagreed in the *Manifesto* was that which he called critical-utopian socialism and communism (p. 99). The thinkers of this category were critical in that they opposed the present conditions that the working classes endured. They were, however, utopian in that their abstract proposals were hopelessly out of touch with the reality of the situation to be faced. The utopians tried to appeal to all classes and to achieve social harmony, thus failing to recognize that class-based antagonism meant that class struggle needed to be recognized as something that could not be avoided.[96]

Before beginning to comment briefly on the ideas and activities of the utopian socialists Marx attempted to clarify his criticism by placing emphasis on a type of thinker that the category should not be assumed to include. The term critical-utopian socialism and communism did not, he stressed, 'refer to that literature which, in every great modern revolution, has always given voice to the demands of the proletariat, such as the writings of Babeuf and others' (p. 99). Marx was, nevertheless, still indisposed to accept the ideas of such thinkers. To appreciate the stance that Marx took in this respect we need thus to look briefly at the ideas of Babeuf.

Gracchus Babeuf was a radical thinker of the sort to which the communist label had traditionally been attached. Active in France in the aftermath of the Revolution in the last few years of the eighteenth century, when the bourgeoisie was already beginning to achieve dominance (or 'sway' as we have seen Marx put it in the *Manifesto*), Babeuf advocated conspiratorial activity. As was discussed earlier in this guide, Marx and Engels would later seek to take communism away from such activity when in the late 1840s they joined and became prominent in the Communist League.

In the *Manifesto* Marx referred to the activities of Babeuf and those influenced by him as the 'first direct attempts of the proletariat to attain its own ends' (p. 99). Babeuf had attempted to put his ideas into practice with an abortive coup d'état in 1795–96. The communism he aimed to introduce would have involved the abolition of private property, which would in turn be followed by the imposition from above, by an authoritarian administration, of absolute economic equality. In this revolutionary society the fruit of all labour would contribute to a central store from which goods would be distributed by the authoritarian leadership he considered necessary.[97]

Attempts such as those inspired by Babeuf, which had taken place at the time when feudalism was in the process of its demise, had failed. According to Marx this was always going to be so for two reasons: first, the proletariat was undeveloped at such times; second, at this stage of the decline of feudalism the economic conditions necessary for the emancipation of the proletariat had not yet materialized. Such conditions could be produced only in the course of the epoch of the bourgeoisie. The two reasons were thus inexorably linked. This, of course, was an analysis consistent with the materialist conception of history.

The first direct attempts of the proletariat to which Marx was referring were, he suggested, accompanied by literature, the character of which was revolutionary but nevertheless at the same time reactionary. The conditions mentioned above in which this movement had arisen meant that this was necessarily the case. This literature, he went on, 'inculcated universal asceticism and social levelling in its crudest form' (p. 99). Although Marx did not elaborate on this short comment, it is an important one that enables us to differentiate Marx's communism from the earlier variant that Babeuf had attempted to introduce. While Marx did not offer a clear and direct statement about the issue of equality in the *Manifesto*, he was by means of this short comment distancing himself from two tenets of what we might call strict egalitarianism. First, his point about crude social levelling illustrates his opposition to doctrine which portrays the condition of equality as having intrinsic value or, in other words, of equality as in itself good whatever the consequences may be. Second, by criticizing the inculcation of universal asceticism he was expressing opposition to unnecessary austerity.

Although at this point the text of the *Manifesto* moves on to consider the ideas of socialists and communists he considered utopian, it is useful to dwell for a moment on Marx's very brief criticism of universal asceticism and crude social levelling just mentioned above. His view can be appreciated if one bears in mind that his idea of a communist society was, indeed, one that emphasized freedom as a key goal. As we have seen, at the end of Section II of the *Manifesto*, having listed the ten measures that should be implemented after the revolution, he stressed that the communists would introduce an association, 'in which the free development of each is the condition for the free development of all' (p. 92). Hence, equality should not be considered intrinsic because that would have meant it would have taken precedence over freedom. To get a better picture of Marx's views on this important part of his political philosophy, and thus put his brief comments into theoretical context, it is useful to turn briefly again to *The German Ideology*, in which he and Engels had recorded their ideas 2 or 3 years before the publication of the *Manifesto*.

In *The German Ideology* Marx and Engels had argued that, at the point at which productive forces would reach an advanced stage, the proletariat would be able to take control over the conditions of their existence by means of revolution. In such conditions the proletarians in their new community would participate as individuals and thus put 'the conditions of the free development and movement of individuals under their control'.[98] Communists, they stressed, were fully aware that egoism was just as much a form of self-assertion, and in some circumstances one that was just as necessary, as was self-sacrifice. Hence, they stressed that Stirner had been wrong to suggest that the communists propose 'to do away with the "private individual" for the sake of the "general", self-sacrificing man'.[99] Here Marx and Engels were defending the communist theory that they were beginning to construct, rather than that of Babeuf. For them, the free development of individuals in the new communist society would be determined by the connection between such individuals. This connection would consist 'partly in the economic prerequisites and partly in the necessary solidarity of the free development of all, and, finally, in the universal character of the activity of individuals on the basis of the existing productive forces'.[100] These thoughts in *The German Ideology* not only locate free development in the material conditions in which the proletariat would necessarily operate, but also help first to illuminate Marx's brief comment in the *Manifesto* about free development, and second to illustrate the gulf between his communism and the austere form that had been advocated by thinkers such as Babeuf.

Having mentioned early communism as a type of thought that should not be confused with critical-utopian socialism and communism, Marx went on in the *Manifesto* to identify some key thinkers who did fit into this utopian category. These were Charles Fourier, Henri-de Saint-Simon and Robert Owen. The systems devised by these three so-called utopians, along with others whom he did not name in the original text, had sprung into existence during the early, undeveloped period of the proletarian class struggle against the bourgeoisie. These early socialists and communists had recognized the existence of class antagonisms of society and the gradual decomposition of the older elements within. They considered, however, that this simply corresponded to the stage of development of industry and the economy that was still relatively secure. While being aware of and deeply concerned with the suffering that the proletariat endured, the utopians could not envisage a process whereby industrial and economic development would provide the opportunity for this exploited class to organize in order to escape from their situation. The utopian socialists had, indeed, failed to see that the proletariat was a newly emerging class which would be able to take the initiative and act on its own behalf (sometimes together with allies) in a revolutionary struggle by which it could take control of society. The interests of the working class would thus need to be cared for, according to the utopians. These thinkers devised plans and systems for such paternalistic purposes.[101] Hence, Marx described Owen, Fourier and Saint-Simon as utopian socialists because they were seeking, without upsetting the rudiments of the existing order, to create conditions in which the interests of the working class could indeed be cared for.

Such schemes devised by the utopians were, in Marx's view, based on the belief that their own personal initiative would prevail over any historical action that the competing classes might take. Conditions of emancipation that were created in the historical process would, in their schemes, be made to yield to conditions which Marx perceived as 'fantastic ones'. The 'gradual, spontaneous class organisation of the proletariat', he went on, would yield 'to an organisation of society especially contrived by these inventors'. History would thus be resolved 'into the propaganda and the practical carrying out of their social plans' (p. 99).

The utopian socialists were indeed very ambitious and creative in building their systems. Marx remarked on the self-confidence of these thinkers, suggesting that they believed such systems would serve the interests of all in society rather than merely those of a particular class. He was particularly scathing of this belief, suggesting that in reality it would serve the interests of the existing dominant class because it would discourage the proletariat from working towards a revolution. In his attempt to imply that they were too concerned with benefits for each member of society to apply the necessary focus, Marx suggested that the socialists whom he placed in this category 'consider themselves far superior to all class antagonisms' (p. 100). This was perhaps a little unfair given the plans of the utopians for the emerging working class.

Whether or not one does consider Marx to have been unfair, his reason for making the comment becomes clearer when one remembers that he and Engels considered the class antagonisms to be so intense and deep rooted that only social and economic change of a fundamental and comprehensive nature could resolve them. Hence, as one contemplates what Marx had to say about the utopian socialists, it will be useful at this point to take a very brief look at what, according to Engels and himself, this type of socialist hoped to achieve, which was somewhat less than such root-and-branch revolutionary change. Useful for this purpose are two footnotes that Engels added to editions of the *Manifesto* that were published after the death of Marx. These footnotes also reveal the identity of one of the 'others' whom Marx had included along with Owen, Fourier and Saint-Simon.

Engels' footnotes each followed Marx's suggestion that the utopians 'still dream of experimental realisation of their social Utopias, of founding isolated "phalanstères," of establishing "Home Colonies," or setting up a "Little Icaria"' (pp. 100–101). Engels' corresponding footnote to the 1888 English edition elaborated as follows: '*Phalanstères* were Socialist colonies on the plan of Charles Fourier; *Icaria* was the name given by Cabet to his Utopia and, later on, to his American Communist colony' (p. 101). Cabet was thus one among them. In the note that he added to the 1890 German edition Engels identified 'Home Colonies' as 'what Owen called his Communist model societies' and elaborated slightly on his earlier comment on phalanstères by saying that this was the name for public palaces that Fourier had planned. Finally, in the 1890 footnote, Engels elaborated on the earlier brief mention of Cabet by stating that '*Icaria* was the name given to the Utopian land of fancy, whose Communist institutions Cabet portrayed' (p. 101). Engels did not mention Saint-Simon, perhaps because the latter utopian thinker did not attempt to build a new community within the old. Saint-Simon had presented his radical views on the problems of unfettered individualism, the importance of the organization of society by experts and equality of opportunity without sufficient substantial views on how to achieve such an organized society. Marx and Engels, of course, considered views on the achievement of broad and extensive social transformation to be crucial to any realistic plan for the necessary extent of revolutionary change.

Marx suggested in the *Manifesto* that the utopian socialists 'reject all political, and especially all revolutionary action', and that 'they wish to attain their ends, by peaceful means, necessarily doomed to failure, and by the force of example, to pave the way for the new social Gospel' (p. 100). This is a sentence that almost invites confusion. The government of communes or broader organization of society led by experts would, according to many people's interpretations, indeed be political. If one purpose of such developments would be to serve as a force of example then this once again may be seen as politics in action. This lack of clarity can, however, be resolved when we consider that in a number of his writings Marx associated politics more specifically with class struggle and competition.[102] This helps put his comment that the utopians rejected political action into context. As has been discussed throughout this guide so far, in 1848 Marx and Engels believed that the time was approaching at which such action could and should be revolutionary. Owen, Fourier, Saint-Simon, Cabet and their like were, Marx believed, utopian for thinking that their new societies could be built without 'political' and indeed revolutionary action.

The utopians had presented their ideas in the earlier decades of the nineteenth century. If we think back to Marx's insistence on the importance of the development of productive forces, which he expressed so powerfully in Section I of the *Manifesto*, his view that such forces were reaching the point at which they would burst asunder the bourgeois mode of production is significant. This is because the ability of the proletariat to mount a successful revolution was being strengthened accordingly. His thought having been guided by this materialist conception of history, Marx was compelled to actually excuse the utopians for painting their 'fantastic pictures of a future society' (p. 100). Such blueprints had, he conceded, been produced during the years in which the proletariat was at an early stage of development. Such fantastic pictures thus corresponded 'with the first instinctive yearnings of that class for a general reconstruction of society' (p. 100).

Marx, furthermore, accepted that the utopians should be given credit where this was due, and this was for the critical element of their thought. They had attacked all the principles of the existing society and were thus able to enlighten the working class to that degree. Ideas and topics which had been voiced by thinkers among this category included (a) the abolition of the town/country distinction, of the family, of the operation of industries for the account of private individuals, and of the wage system; (b) the assertion of social harmony; and (c) the use of the state simply to supervise production for the purpose of such harmony. These ideas and topics served to indicate that there could be alternatives to the present system of class antagonisms – antagonisms that may disappear if a new system were to be built. Nevertheless, such antagonisms were 'recognised in their earliest indistinct and undefined forms only' (p. 100), and the alternatives would likewise be relatively undeveloped. The proposals had thus not been accompanied by the recognition of the extent and entirety that the antagonisms would reach in the years approaching 1848. The utopians did not, moreover, as mentioned above, appreciate the magnitude or revolutionary nature of the action that, according to Marx and Engels, would be required to overcome them. This problem thus, for them, served to render the proposals purely utopian in character.

Having acknowledged that the weaknesses in utopian socialist and communist thought rested at least in part upon the conditions in which its authors operated, Marx was not yet finished with those he placed in this category. After the brief acknowledgement of the good intentions he resumed his incisive criticism, stating that the significance of utopian ideas bore 'an inverse relationship to historical development' (p. 100). For him, any value or theoretical justification that the critical element of the utopian thought may have had when applied to the early stages of the class antagonisms diminished as the class struggles developed and began to take shape. Hence, although when the utopian pioneers had presented their ideas they did have a revolutionary air about them, the same could not be said of their disciples who rehearsed the same ideas later. Those rehearsals took place when the proletariat had developed further and was approaching the position at which the dominant class could be challenged. In the hands of the disciples utopianism had thus become reactionary in character as its ideas served 'to deaden the class struggle and to reconcile the class antagonisms' (p. 100). He dismissed the phalanstères, home colonies and 'Little Icaria' as 'castles in the air' and 'duodecimo editions of the New Jerusalem' (pp. 100–1). By the latter he meant little and second-rate editions of blueprints for a new society. The bourgeoisie would not allow the full development of new societies if they believed such developments would challenge their dominance. Hence, in order to succeed at all, such schemes needed to appeal to the feelings and purses of that dominant class. 'By degrees', he suggested, 'they sink into the category of the reactionary [or] conservative Socialists depicted above' (p. 101).

A theme that is present throughout Marx's criticism of the various socialist and communist writers and groups of the period from the end of the eighteenth century to the mid-nineteenth century is that of the necessity for the proletariat to engage in class struggle and thus bring about the new society. Although he did of course consider that members of the Communist League, not least Engels and himself, would play a leading role in guiding the class struggle, the workers themselves would need to play a part in releasing themselves from the exploitation they faced in the epoch of the bourgeoisie. The need for proletarian revolution was thus one of the most distinctive features of the *Manifesto*. Indeed, in an influential article of the 1970s, Robin Blackburn went so far as to suggest that the theory of proletarian revolution was the decisive contribution that Marx and Engels brought to the workers' movement and radical political thought, distinguishing them from earlier thinkers and activists.[103] Whether or not one agrees with Blackburn that the theory of proletarian revolution stands above all other features of Marxism in terms of significance, as one reads the *Manifesto* it becomes clear that it is certainly a crucial element of the pamphlet.

Marx brought the section to a close with the following single-sentence paragraph: 'The Owenites in England, and the Fourierists in France, respectively, oppose the Chartists and the *Réformistes*' (p. 101). Some insight into the latter group was offered by Engels in his footnote to the 1888 English edition. They were republican democrats who contributed to the French radical newspaper *La Réforme* and were, as Engels put it, 'more or less tinged with socialism' (p. 101). Given the invective with which Marx had criticized such mild socialists in the previous section of the *Manifesto*, why this group was mentioned favourably at this stage in the pamphlet may seem curious. Some light will be thrown on this in the next section of this guide. Turning to the other group he mentioned the Chartists were a British group who campaigned for a range of measures for working-class people, including the suffrage, in the early to mid-nineteenth century. The purpose of Marx's reference to the Chartists likewise becomes clearer in his next section, which also helps clarify a point he had made about collaboration with other parties in his Section II.

Study questions

1 Why did Marx use the term 'Feudal Socialists' to refer to the aristocrats who criticized bourgeois society?

2 What did Marx identify as a major weakness in the thought of Sismondi?

3 What did Marx consider to be fundamentally wrong with the arguments of the true socialists?

4 Why did Marx place Proudhon into the conservative or bourgeois category of socialism?

5 What, in Marx's view, was wrong with the communism of Babeuf?

6 Why did Marx refer to the ideas of Owen, Fourier, Saint-Simon and Cabet as utopian?

7 What did Marx consider to be wrong with utopian socialism?

8 How does Marx's discussion of socialist literature help clarify his reference to French radicals in the preamble?

'Position of the communists in relation to the various existing opposition parties'

Marx began the fourth, final main section of the *Manifesto* with the statement that Section II had clarified the relations of the communists with other working-class parties of the period. In that second section he had, however, perhaps rather frustratingly for readers, refrained from offering examples. Such frustration will be lifted when one reads his statement at the beginning of Section IV that the Chartists in England and agrarian reformers were such examples. Taking up from where he left his brief comment about the Chartists at the end of Section III, in this final section he offered this group of British activists, along with the American agrarian reformers and French *Réformistes* among others, as examples of working-class parties with which the Communists could build relations (p. 101).

The American agrarian reformers campaigned for laws to protect small farmers by excusing them from rent and limiting the size of large farms.[104] The Chartists were, however, perhaps the more significant in that they were coming to be prominent in the minds of Marx and Engels as an example of the sort of party with which, they believed, the communists should work. Engels made this quite clear in his answer to Question 25 of his second draft: 'Principles of Communism'. The question itself asked, in words that clearly resemble those used by Marx for the title of Section IV of the *Manifesto*, what was 'the attitude of the communists to the other political parties of our time'? As part of his catechetical reply Engels said that 'the working-class Chartists are indefinitely closer to the communists than the democratic petty bourgeoisie or the so-called Radicals'.[105]

Engels in particular was indeed very sympathetic to the aims and activities of the Chartists, even though he thought that something more than they had to offer would be required in order to achieve a new, acceptable society.[106] He and Marx did in fact establish links with some prominent members of the Chartist movement. Moreover, the Chartists published some of the works of Marx and Engels, including the first English translation of the *Manifesto*, in their newspapers. Marx and Engels would continue to take an interest in the activities of the Chartists, especially the more radical figures in the movement such as Ernest Jones, throughout the 1850s.[107]

This discussion of relations between the communists and other working-class parties is hugely important with regard to what was, as mentioned earlier, one of the main themes of the *Manifesto*. This theme was the necessity for the proletariat to harness the opportunity to engage in revolutionary action. This would be required in order to replace the capitalist mode of production with a new one that would eventually lead to a communist society. The proletariat would thus be harnessing the productive forces to achieve results that the fetters imposed by the capitalist mode of production had hitherto precluded. The collaboration with other parties was necessary in various countries in order to prepare the ground for the revolutionary action. 'The Communists', he insisted, fight for the attainment of the immediate aims, for the enforcement of the momentary interests of the working class' (p. 101). Such collaboration was needed at this stage – a stage which he called 'the movement of the present' (p. 101). He went on to add the crucial point that the communists 'also represent and take care of the future of that movement' (p. 101).

In order to fulfil the responsibility for the future of the movement Marx considered it vitally important to maintain control over any such alliances with other parties during the movement of the present. Here he mentioned the links the communists were establishing in France with the Social-Democrats. As is made clear in Engels' second footnote to the 1888 English edition of the *Manifesto*, this was the parliamentary wing, led by Louis Blanc, of the socialist-tinged *Réformistes* (p. 101). Marx, one may recall, had mentioned this French group a couple of paragraphs earlier, at the end of Section III of the pamphlet. This alliance had been established, Marx informed his readers, in order to oppose the conservative and radical bourgeoisie. This statement by Marx regarding the Social-Democrats, along with that of Engels with regard to the Chartists, illustrates that they considered these two parties to be far more useful to the cause than were the socialists and early communists who had been dismissed in Section III of the pamphlet. Crucially, however, for the future of the movement Marx's communists – those of the Communist League – reserved the right in this alliance 'to take up a critical position in regard to phases and illusions traditionally handed down from the great Revolution' (p. 101).

Marx turned to Switzerland for an example of another ally with which the Communists could work. This was the party to which Marx referred at this point as the Radicals. Engels had in answer to Question 25 of 'Principles of Communism', said that this party was the only group in that country with which the communists could cooperate, but added that it was actually a very mixed party. Among these radicals, he added, 'the Vaudois and Genevese are the most advanced'.[108] By this statement he was referring to the organization of the Radical Party on the basis of the cantons of which the country was comprised. The two cantons to which he was referring were Vaud and Geneva.

Marx too commented, in the final section of the *Manifesto*, on the mixed nature of those gathered under the Radical banner in Switzerland. The communists, he suggested, do not lose sight of the fact that 'this party consists of antagonistic elements, partly of Democratic Socialists, in the French sense, partly of radical bourgeois' (p. 101). Once again, Marx was indicating that the Communists should be alert to problems which this alliance might bring, and to the necessity to remain committed to their cause. Having in the preamble identified French radicals as opponents of communism, he believed that any alliances with groups that may qualify as such must be undertaken with great caution, retaining the aforementioned autonomy by asserting dominance in such relationships.

Continuing his brief summary of alliances the Communists had built, Marx mentioned two examples which illustrate his awareness of, and his plans to address, the different levels of development of the capitalist mode of production in different parts of Europe. As will be discussed in a moment, this is an important point that helps clarify a paragraph that follows shortly afterwards regarding the course that the series of revolutions around the world would take.

The first such example was in Poland where, Marx suggested, the communists insisted on an agrarian revolution. This would be, as he put it, 'the prime condition for national emancipation' (p. 102). The only clue that Marx gave as to which party he meant was that it had fomented the insurrection in the Polish city of Cracow in 1846. In one of his very useful footnotes to his edition of the *Manifesto* Bender identifies this party as the Polish Democratic Society. The emancipation was from Russia, which dominated Poland at the time. The peasantry would need to be involved and the Democratic Society was the party though which this would happen.[109] The question which this raises is that of why such emancipation was thus significant. One can fathom the answer by recalling the guiding thread which, in his 'Preface to *A Critique of Political Economy*', he suggested the *Manifesto* epitomized. This thread, as has been mentioned in a number of points so far in this guide, is the materialist conception of history. Before the proletarian revolution could achieve its aims, the bourgeois mode of production needed to run its course in order to allow the productive forces to develop. Until emancipation from domination by feudal Russia had been achieved the epoch of the bourgeoisie could not begin to take its course.

The second example of an alliance in a relatively undeveloped part of Europe was Germany (which at that time was a confederation of states rather than a unified nation-state). There, according to Marx, the communists fought with (or, in other words, were on the same side as) the bourgeoisie whenever it acted 'in a revolutionary way, against the absolute monarchy, the feudal squirearchy, and the petty bourgeoisie' (p. 102). This is a fairly obvious case of capitalism needing to develop before the proletariat could hope to achieve the sort of communist society in which the productive forces could be allowed to produce abundance for all. Because of this goal, which would of course require the bourgeois epoch to be brought down, Marx went on to stress that the communists would need to ensure that the proletarians remained fully and constantly aware of the hostile antagonism between themselves and the bourgeoisie. This was because the German workers would need to be ready to right away use to their own advantage the social and political conditions that the bourgeoisie would introduce when they themselves achieved supremacy. This would mean that 'after the fall of the reactionary classes in Germany, the fight against the bourgeoisie itself may immediately begin' (p. 102).

These thoughts that Marx offered in the closing stages of the *Manifesto* about the prospects for proletarian revolution have been the subject of much controversy. They have been perceived as inconsistent with a major theme of the pamphlet. This was that, in order for the productive forces to develop sufficiently to create the abundant resources that communism would require, the epoch of the bourgeoisie would need itself to reach an advanced stage. This has been considered inconsistent with Marx's suggestion in the final short section that, rather than endure a lengthy period in which bourgeois power would develop, the proletariat could act at once in Germany. As John Cunliffe discussed in a very useful paper published in the 1980s, this is a controversy essentially over the schedule for revolution. The key question is whether one of the key assumptions of the pamphlet – that proletarian revolution could only succeed in advanced capitalist countries – is consistent with the strategy to push for the revolution in undeveloped Germany. The view that consistency was lacking came to be prominent in debates about the *Manifesto*.[110]

Cunliffe helped resolve this apparent problem of inconsistency by noting that Marx emphasized strongly that there was an international dimension of capitalism. Countries at various stages of economic and political development interacted with one another. Germany was thus a part of an interconnected international economic system in which, one may recall from this guide's discussion of the first main section of the *Manifesto*, production and consumption in each country had a cosmopolitan character. Germany could undergo proletarian revolution but only as part of an international movement. The main theme of the pamphlet, particularly of Part I, concerns very general tendencies, one of which is that international action was, hence, necessary for the introduction of communism. Marx was not clear or unambiguous on the detail of the situation required for a proletarian revolution to succeed in backward Germany. Nevertheless, as Cunliffe suggests, Marx seems to have been implying that 'a revolution in a backward country could succeed only by acting as a precursor of successful revolutions in advanced ones'.[111]

The paragraph of the *Manifesto* that presents the ambiguous position regarding Germany is followed by one which offers a clue that Marx was indeed implying the point that Cunliffe attributes to him. Marx stated in the latter paragraph two reasons to urge the communists to attend chiefly to Germany. The first reason was as follows: that country was on the eve of a bourgeois revolution that would, one could be certain, be carried out under more advanced conditions of European civilization and with a more developed proletariat than had been the case in England and France during the seventeenth and eighteenth centuries respectively (p. 102). The point about advanced conditions of European civilization illustrates the international aspect that Marx considered so important. Engels perhaps put it more clearly in his second draft, in response to Question 19, which asked whether it would be possible for the revolution to take place in a single country. Engels said that this would not be possible. In creating the world market big industry had brought the world's peoples into close relationships, meaning that there was interdependence between them, with the result that the actions of each had effects on the others.[112]

Another significant point within this first of the two reasons is that, although Germany was backward, it was a part of the international system that was driven by the more advanced countries within which the productive forces had been nurtured. As it was emerging within this system wherein production and consumption in each country had a cosmopolitan character, the German proletariat was relatively well advanced, even though it lagged behind its counterparts in countries such as England and France. Engels' answer to Question 19 in the final draft helps clarify this point too (although his use of the term 'civilized peoples' is rather insulting and patronizing to people in countries that he did not consider as such). Big industry had 'coordinated the social development of the civilized countries to such an extent that, in all of them, bourgeoisie and proletariat have become the decisive classes and the struggle between them the great struggle of the day'.[113] He included Germany in his list of 'civilized' countries.

Marx's second reason why the communists should turn their attention to Germany actually reiterated the point he had made in the previous paragraph of his final section. This was that the bourgeois revolution in that country would be 'but the prelude to an immediately following proletarian revolution' (p. 102). Engels' reply to Question 19 in the final draft helps clarify why this would be so. The revolution would, he suggested, develop in the more advanced countries 'more or less rapidly, according as one country or the other has a more developed industry, greater wealth, a more significant mass of productive forces'. The revolution would, he went on, 'go slowest and will meet most obstacles in Germany'. It would go 'most rapidly and with the fewest difficulties in England'. The revolution would thereafter impact powerfully on the other countries of the world, which followed countries such as England where capitalism was most developed. Regarding the other countries of the world, it would 'radically alter the course of development which they have followed up to now, while greatly stepping up its pace'.[114]

Engels' comments were significant. Although he saw Germany as one of the more advanced economies, his comment about other countries thus not being applicable directly, Germany would still feel the impact of the rapid development in England. As the course of development would be altered the proletariat itself would develop more quickly accordingly. Marx's comment about the German proletariat can be seen in this light, as can his suggestion that the revolution in some countries would serve as the precursor of successful ones elsewhere.

Marx drew the *Manifesto* to a close with some brief comments which serve to clarify what he had already said about the position of the communists in relation to other parties. Any revolutionary movement that was to campaign against 'the existing social and political order of things' (p. 102) would receive the support of the communists. As they gave that support the communists would 'bring to the front, as the leading question in each, the property question, no matter what its degree of development at the time' (p. 102). They would also strive to bring the democratic parties of all the countries to union and agreement.

If this enthusiasm for democracy appears to show that Marx was pulling back from his revolutionary approach, then one should remember that in 1848 the campaign for democracy was itself a radical position to take. Also significant is the purpose which, in Marx's view, democracy should serve. Democracy was not, for him, the ultimate aim of the revolution but, rather, a forum within which the class struggle should be pursued. As was discussed earlier in this guide, he expected the proletarians, led by the communists, to win the battle of democracy.

The communists, Marx stressed, would not conceal their views and aims in this battle of democracy. Their approach would be to declare openly that what they aimed to achieve was the overthrow by force of all the existing social conditions that he had criticized so powerfully in the pamphlet. Indeed, as was mentioned earlier in this guide, Marx and Engels had helped to steer the Communist League away from its previous conspiratorial approach into one of open campaigning. 'Let the ruling classes tremble', Marx demanded in line with this new approach, 'at a Communist revolution' (p. 102). Earlier in the *Manifesto* Marx had, it will be recalled, suggested that the economic and social conditions of the proletariat would continue to deteriorate as the bourgeoisie responded to the crisis by increasing the exploitation on which their power and wealth rested. With this in mind Marx stressed that the proletarians had 'nothing to lose but their chains'. The proletariat did, however, he went on, 'have a world to win' (p. 102). In other words, as the revolutionary struggle was an international one, the proletariat would upon their victory gain what he had earlier in the pamphlet referred to as political sway over a society which had, in the epoch of the bourgeoisie, become a global one. It was from this internationalist position that Marx's famous slogan is offered in capital letters at the end of the pamphlet: 'WORKING MEN OF ALL COUNTRIES, UNITE!' (p. 102).

How this famous work of revolutionary advocacy, social comment and political philosophy was received both in Marx and Engels' time and by the later generations of activists and intellectuals will be discussed in the next chapter of this guide. Before that, however, the final section of the present chapter will turn to a range of prefaces that were attached to the *Manifesto* as it was published in various languages later in the nineteenth century. These prefaces appear in many later editions. This will help show how Marx and Engels reflected on the pamphlet as their thought developed and as they experienced the decades after 1848.

Study questions

1 Why did Marx insist that the communists should work with some other political parties?

2 Why did Marx consider it so important to maintain control over any such alliances with other parties during what he called 'the movement of the present'?

3 Why did Marx say that an agrarian revolution would be necessary in Poland?

4 How, in Marx's view, could the proletarian revolution be successful in relatively undeveloped Germany?

5 For what reasons, according to Marx, would the communists strive to bring the democratic parties of all the countries to union and agreement?

6 Why did Marx suggest that, in embarking on the revolutionary struggle, the proletarians had nothing to lose but their chains?

7 Why did Marx suggest that the proletarians had a world to win?

Prefaces to various language editions

The prefaces often attached to the later editions of the *Manifesto* include two that were originally published before the death of Marx in 1883, as well as several that accompanied the editions that appeared over the following 10 years before Engels' death in 1895. These prefaces largely, as one might expect, defended the views that Marx had expressed in the pamphlet. In that respect there is much in those prefaces that is not particularly remarkable or profound. There are, however, some interesting comments that illustrate the ways in which Marx and Engels thought that the work may have been revised had it been written later than 1848. It is therefore worthwhile to focus on these later prefaces. The first was written by Marx and Engels for an edition that appeared in German in 1872.

Preface to the German edition of 1872

Marx and Engels' preface of 1872 begins by stating what sort of organization the Communist League was: essentially an association of workers organized internationally. The League had, the authors declared in the first paragraph, decided that a theoretical and practical programme needed to be produced, which was what the *Manifesto* provided. This acknowledgement of the theoretical and practical elements of the pamphlet confirms what has been said in the present guide about the work having a dual purpose: philosophical and political. The first paragraph also mentions the different editions in which the pamphlet had hitherto been published in a range of languages, serving thus to illustrate the international scope of the audience that the authors targeted.

The preface goes on to state that although there had been great political changes and other developments during the 25 years since the original edition had been published, the general principles of the work remained the same. The only improvements that would be made were it to be rewritten would involve changes to some of the details in a few places. Marx and Engels then made a brief but very important statement. No special stress, they suggested, should now 'be laid on the revolutionary measures proposed at the end of Section II' (p. 103). This was because the manner in which the principles would need to be applied in practice would always depend upon the historical conditions of the particular time. The *Manifesto*, they stressed, itself stated this. Conditions in industry had changed, as had the organizational capacity of the working class. Hence, that passage at the end of Section II would have been 'very differently worded' (p. 103) had it been written in the early 1870s. This raises the question of the way in which those conditions had changed and how correspondingly the organizing capacity of the working class had been transformed.

What one needs to grasp in order to appreciate what Marx and Engels meant is that, in a number of his works written between the *Manifesto* and this new preface of 1872, Marx had been concerned with the consolidation of industry into fewer, larger units. Productive forces had become so advanced that this development was needed in order to get the most from their capacity to increase production. What was thus happening was that the forces were having a structural effect in that the change was not necessarily being planned by individual people. This in turn was having another structural effect in that the conditions were being created which were conducive to cooperative forms of work, which served to unite and train people in their organizational capacity. The revolt of the working classes was almost being expedited by the structural processes at work in that the productive forces were becoming incompatible with private industry. This process coincided with the crises that worsened the conditions of an increasingly exploited proletariat with an enhanced organizational capacity. The revolt of this class was thus drawing nearer.[115] This process can be seen in terms of the working out of contradictions which was discussed earlier in the present guide.

Returning to the text of the 1872 preface, immediately after this brief mention of the changing industrial conditions and the enhanced organizational capacity of the working classes, Marx and Engels wrote that the working class had thus begun to enjoy practical experience similar to that which had helped bring about the February Revolution. As it had also been named in such terms with this effect in *The Class Struggles in France*, we can assume that they meant the revolution that broke out in France just as the *Manifesto* was being finished early in 1848.[116] Still more than the February Revolution, they went on, the Paris Commune of 1871, 'where the proletariat for the first time held political power for two whole months' (p. 103), had rendered the programme at the end of Section II of the *Manuscript*, antiquated.

The Commune to which Marx and Engels were referring was the community set up in Paris at the end of the Franco-Prussian War, as the city was under siege by the Prussian army. Various working-class groups were represented in the cooperatives, committees and other organizations of which this system of popular governance was comprised. France having just lost the war, the new government now had to deal with the Commune. They did so ruthlessly, sending in troops that slaughtered thousands of people.[117] Marx and Engels considered the Commune to be very significant. It had, they conceded, proved that notwithstanding the organizational advancements, the working class was unable to seize the existing state machinery and wield it for the purposes of establishing working-class control of society (p. 103).

Marx and Engels also suggested in this 1872 preface that what Marx had said in Section IV of the *Manifesto* about relations between the communists and other opposition parties remained in principle correct. Nevertheless, as the political situation had changed so much since 1848, and with many of those parties having been 'swept from off the earth' by 'the progress of history' (p. 104),

Marx's comments on them had in practice become antiquated. They concluded the preface by suggesting that the *Manifesto* was now in effect a historical document, but added that a subsequent edition may perhaps appear with a new introduction which would discuss the changes that had happened since the original pamphlet had been written. While such an edition would never actually appear, a number of new prefaces would, as mentioned earlier, be appended to the *Manifesto* over the remaining years of the nineteenth century, including one to a Russian edition of 1882.

Preface to the Russian edition of 1882

The preface to this Russian edition was, like that to the German edition of 1872, written jointly by Marx and Engels. The first edition to appear in this language had, they noted, been translated by Michael Bakunin (a prominent anarchist with whom Marx had engaged in intense rivalry) and published in the 1860s. The West, Marx and Engels suggested, would have seen this original Russian edition as nothing more than a 'literary curiosity' (p. 104). Indeed, as the remainder of the preface indicates, just as in 1848 Russia certainly did not appear to be sufficiently developed for the text of the *Manifesto* to have any relevance to that country at all, this had until very recently seemed to be the likely state of affairs for the foreseeable future. This was because Russia was 'the last great reserve of all European reaction' (p. 104). Its main roles in the international capitalist system being those of a source of raw materials and a market for the industrial products of the more advanced countries, Russia was, not unlike the United States of America, in effect a pillar of the existing European system. The proletariat was in this state of development barely significant. This, however, was a situation that, in the view of Marx and Engels, seemed to be changing. The reactionary role of the Tsar as a force of intervention to maintain the old order in Europe was now being undermined by revolutionary pressure in his own country.

In the case of the United States mass immigration from Europe meant that agriculture and industry were developing so rapidly in this relatively new country that it would soon be in a position to challenge the monopoly position of England and the other developed countries of Western Europe. Regarding agriculture in the United

States, Marx and Engels identified a similar process to that which Marx had discussed regarding the advanced capitalist countries in the main text of the *Manifesto*, whereby small enterprises were being swallowed up by the larger ones. A massive concentration was taking place in the United States along with the development of a mass industrial proletariat.

The developments that Marx and Engels identified in Russia and the United States can be seen to fit, albeit not entirely comfortably, with the materialist conception of history with which the *Manifesto* had (without using the term) been concerned. Marx and Engels now recognized that the developments in those countries would have particular consequences for the people and classes within them. The process of the rise and decline of bourgeois society would be likely to take place in Russia and the United States within a considerably compressed timescale with characteristics peculiar to each of them.

With bourgeois property just beginning to develop rapidly in Russia, Marx and Engels identified what they called the 'capitalist swindle' (p. 105). This was a reference to the key point in the *Manifesto* of exploitation in class relations. In this respect the guiding thread of the materialist conception of history is in evidence, because the bourgeois class was gaining power as productive forces developed. Nevertheless, they also recognized another phenomenon that did not fit comfortably in the pattern that the materialist conception outlined. This was that in Russia more than half the land was owned collectively by the peasants. This traditional Russian form of communal ownership was the *obshchina* or, in other words, village commune. Marx and Engels considered carefully whether the process of development through which the Western European countries had passed would be followed with revisions or alternatively avoided. Could, they asked, 'the Russian *obshchina*, though greatly undermined, yet a form of primeval common ownership of land, pass directly to the higher form of Communist common ownership?' (p. 105). One can see that, if so, the process of the materialist conception of history would indeed be broken. 'Or, on the contrary', they went on, 'must it first pass through the same process of dissolution such as constitutes the historical evolution of the West?' (p. 105). They thus expressed uncertainty whether the latter course would need to be the case for the historical development to be consistent with the process in question.

In fact, however, if one considers carefully Marx's discussion of the prospects for revolution in undeveloped Germany at the end of the original text of the *Manifesto*, it is evident that he and Engels had already perceived situations whereby future developments would deviate from the path his main argument had anticipated. They were, in this 1882 preface, considering the possibilities of another such deviation. As was the case in their discussion of prospects in Germany, the international element of their doctrine is of crucial importance in this respect. If revolution did break out in Russia this could serve as the signal for proletarian revolution in the West. If the Russian and Western revolutions were to complement one another, they suggested, 'the present Russian ownership of land may serve as the starting point for a communist development' (p. 105). Marx died the following year and so would not, of course, observe whether developments in Russia would substantiate this prediction (and as it turned out successful revolutions did not take place in Western Europe, even though the Russian revolution of 1917 did bring the communists into power in that country until 1991). Indeed, the preface to the German edition published in 1883 was written by Engels alone.

Preface to the German edition of 1883

Engels began this German edition by lamenting the death of Marx, noting that his comrade's body rested at Highgate Cemetery (in a grave which, incidentally, with its huge monument later erected, visitors to London can still go to see today). There could now, Engels conceded, 'be even less thought of revising or supplementing the Manifesto' (p. 105). He went on to suggest, with excessive modesty given that he had written the drafts that contained many of the key points, that 'the basic thought running through the Manifesto . . . belongs solely and exclusively to Marx' (pp. 105–6). Engels wrote a brief summary in this preface to Marx's 'basic thought' that is actually quite useful to readers for the purpose of revision. The summary outlines clearly the argument of the pamphlet in terms of the guiding thread that Marx had presented in the 'Preface to *A Critique of Political Economy*' in 1859. This helps substantiate Marx's claim in that preface that the *Manifesto* was part of the wider project of presenting that guiding thread.

Beginning his summary Engels said the *Manifesto* held that 'economic production, and the structure of society of every historical epoch necessarily arising therefrom, constitute the foundation for the political and intellectual history of that epoch' (pp. 105–106). This serves as a clear statement of the process of the guiding thread or, in other words, of the materialist conception of history. The economic structure at the base and the political and intellectual superstructure resting upon it are clearly represented in that statement.

Engels went on to mention another feature of Marx's basic thought that followed from the one he had just considered; this was 'that consequently (ever since the dissolution of the primaeval communal ownership of land) all history has been a history of class struggles' (p. 106). As the present and previous chapters of this guide have discussed, this focus on class struggle as a key element in history was indeed an important theme of the *Manifesto*. Engels elaborated by stating that this history of class struggles was one of 'struggles between exploited and exploiting, between dominated and dominating classes at various stages of social evolution' (p. 106).

Engels finished his brief account of Marx's basic thought by noting its key revolutionary element. The proletariat was exploited and oppressed by the bourgeoisie. Marx, he stressed, held that the class struggle had 'reached a stage where the exploited and oppressed class . . . can no longer emancipate itself from the class which exploits and oppresses it . . . without at the same time forever freeing the whole of society from exploitation, oppression, class struggles' (p. 106).

Engels said that it was now time for this summary, which as he suggested he had expressed many times, 'to stand in front of the *Manifesto* itself' (p. 106). It thus became the new preface. As mentioned earlier, his summary provides a valuable statement of the guiding thread that Marx considered the *Manifesto* to express. As will now be discussed, the next of the prefaces that have come to traditionally accompany editions of the pamphlet was rather different.

Preface to the English edition of 1888

Unlike the 1883 German preface with its quite specific purpose, the one by Engels for the English-language edition of the *Manifesto* published in 1888 was far less focused, offering a looser set of comments. This English preface began by offering a brief history of the *Manifesto* to date, focusing on the publication of the first edition and the environment of the European Left in which the pamphlet's message was received in the years and decades that followed. Following the defeat of the 1848 revolutions, Engels noted, proletarian movements in countries such as France and Prussia faced ruthless suppression, including lengthy prison sentences. Those members of the Communist League who had avoided arrest formally dissolved the organization. The *Manifesto* 'seemed henceforth doomed to oblivion' (p. 107).

Engels wrote that when the organized European workers had recovered from the disappointments of 1848 the International Working Men's Association (now known as the First International) was formed in 1864. In attempting to represent a broad and diverse movement the association needed to be attractive to all the groupings within it. Marx had drawn up the programme for it with such necessity in view. Engels suggested that by the time it had broken up 10 years later, the different factions had indeed begun to dissolve and the principles of the *Manifesto* were once more becoming attractive, making 'considerable headway among the working men of all countries' (p. 107).

A grasp of the latter point requires a little attention to context. The First International was riven with divisions such as those between revolutionaries and reformists throughout its short lifespan. Moreover, Marx, who tended to argue for reform in the short term in order to prepare the way for revolution, was often supported by the moderate English trade unionists. The more radical members of secret societies sought to foment European-wide insurrections.[118] The radical factions had lost influence by the time of the break-up of the First International. While the principles of the *Manifesto* may furthermore, as Engels suggested, have 'made considerable headway among the working men of all countries' (p. 107), Marx himself had stepped back from the urgency that the pages of the pamphlet had conveyed. Engels reported in this preface that an English trade union leader announced that '[c]ontinental socialism has lost its terror for us' (p. 107). Perhaps this was because, as represented by Marx who as just mentioned had gained the support of English unions, continental socialism included a clear role for parliamentary politics. Marx had indeed, after the *Manifesto*, placed far more emphasis on parliamentary means to the eventual communist ends.[119] Hence, the pamphlet was now less likely than before to instil fear in the trade unionists.

As Engels went on to mention, the influence of the *Manifesto* had, after the failure of the 1848 and the repression that followed, now come 'to the front again' (p. 107). It had, indeed, by the time Engels wrote this preface, been published many times and in many countries. While there is no need to reproduce it here, some readers may be interested to turn to Engels list in the 1888 preface of a number of those editions (pp. 107–8).

Engels turned next to the socialist/communist differentiation that was discussed earlier in the present guide. As he suggested, given that he and Marx had sought the demise of capitalism and profit, the *Manifesto* could certainly not have been called a socialist one at the time it was written. This was because 'socialism' was considered a middle-class, respectable doctrine that tinkered at the edges of the existing economic system, posing no real challenge to it. The utopian systems of the Owenites and Fourierists were examples of the respectable socialism. Engels was thus saying nothing really new.

The preface moved on to a different topic as Engels offered a brief summary of the fundamental proposition or, in other words, the core argument, of the *Manifesto* – an argument that, as has often been stressed in this guide, has come to be known as the materialist conception of history. He was perhaps once again a little too modest, saying that the proposition belonged to Marx who had worked out and put before him in clear terms the argument that he was himself progressing towards in 'Conditions of the Working Class in England' (p. 109) (which was the book usually published in English as *The Condition of the Working Class in England*).

Engels brought the preface to a close with a very long quote from the German edition of 1872, basically saying as he had in the preface to the latter edition that the basic principles of the *Manifesto* remained the same as at the time of the original publication. Finally, he acknowledged that Moore was the translator of Marx's pamphlet for this edition and that he and Moore had 'revised it in common' (p. 110). This final comment of the preface is quite important because this is of course the translation used in the edition on which this guide focuses and indeed in most other English-language editions. Engels' comment at the end of the preface of 1888 helps confirm that the text of that translation is reasonably accurate to the original intentions and presentation of Marx and himself. As mentioned in several places in this guide, however, the Carver translation does sometimes help make the intentions clearer. This preface is followed by one for an edition published in Germany 2 years later.

Preface to the German edition of 1890

The preface to the German edition of 1890 actually contains little that will help readers to understand the text of the *Manifesto* or its context. There is indeed not much at all in this preface that should be considered either new or highly significant at all. Much of it simply repeats the detailed discussion of previous editions of the pamphlet. It is, therefore, not necessary to focus on the text of this preface until the final two paragraphs – the second of which consists of only one short sentence.

Engels began the penultimate paragraph by conceding that, when the *Manifesto* was originally published, few voices responded to the call for working men of all countries to unite, even though this was 'on the eve of the first Paris Revolution in which the proletariat came out with the demand of its own' (p. 113). He was thus, indirectly, suggesting that in the famous revolution of 1789 and also in the lesser-celebrated 1930 revolution the workers had not worked on their own behalf but, rather, helped the campaign for the demands of the bourgeoisie.

Engels continued the paragraph with the claim that the formation in 1864 of the International Working Men's Association represented the internationalization of the workers' movement. The influence of this event, he went on, was still being felt as he wrote, even though the International had been in existence only for 9 years and was thus now extinct. As evidence of this influence he offered an example that allowed him to restate the support that he and Marx had always given to campaigns for a shorter working day.

Marx and Engels had, in the *Manifesto*, placed great emphasis on the Ten Hours Act as a major achievement of the British workers' movement. In this preface of 1890 Engels was excited concerning the prospects of gaining international agreement to reduce still further the hours that employers could demand of their workers.

There had been pressure for such agreement in 1866 by the Geneva Congress of the International and in 1889 by the Paris Workers' Congress. Having played a leading role in organizing the latter congress in 1888 and the early months of 1889 Engels had travelled to France to attend the event in July.

Thanks to Engels' contribution to the organization of the conference it was attended by nearly 400 delegates of left-wing parties from 20 countries. He left the conference with confidence in the potential of the international movement to make progress on a range of issues.[120] His confidence can be clearly seen in the 1890 preface. Even as he was writing it, he declared, the European and American proletariat was preparing to campaign in unison 'for *one* (the emphasis is in the original) immediate aim: the standard eight-hour working day to be established by legal enactment' (p. 113). The eyes of landlords and capitalists of all countries would be opened to such proletarian unity. He ended the preface with the following thought: 'If only Marx were still by my side to see this with his own eyes' (p. 113). Two years later he wrote a preface to a Polish edition in which his optimism continued to be visible, even if his excitement had waned.

Preface to the Polish edition of 1892

In comparison with the high-spirited end to the 1890 German preface, the beginning of Engels' 1892 preface to the Polish edition was rather formal and dry. The *Manifesto*, he suggested, 'has become an index, as it were, of the development of large-scale industry on the European continent' (p. 113). What he meant, he elaborated, was that in a given country as industry expands so in proportion does the growth of the demand among workers 'for enlightenment regarding their position as the working class in relation to the possessing classes' (p. 113). In proportion to this demand the socialist movement spreads among the workers and, in turn, in proportion to this 'the demand for the Manifesto increases' (p. 113). Both the condition of the labour movement and the degree of development of large-scale industry could, he claimed in interpretation of this series of correlations, 'be measured with fair accuracy in every country by the number of copies of the Manifesto circulated in the language of that country' (pp. 113–4).

Engels' reference to an index and his claim of 'fair accuracy' should not be taken too literally. He actually admitted as much by inserting the key words 'as it were' (meaning 'so to speak' or 'as if this were really the case') after 'has become an index'. To grasp why he would want to use such rhetoric one must remember that this was a preface to a political pamphlet, a manifesto. Engels went on, for the remainder of this preface, to discuss Poland as an example to illustrate the index thesis – understandably of course given his intended readership for the edition.

Engels' discussion of the situation in Poland in 1892 indicates that there had been significant economic progress in that country since Marx had briefly mentioned the campaign for an agrarian revolution in the final section of the *Manifesto*. It also indicates that there had been little or nothing that could be described as political progress. The Kingdom of Poland was created in 1815 by the Congress of Vienna and was thus informally known as Congress Poland. The kingdom was, as we saw earlier, dominated and in fact ruled by Russia. After several revolts against Russian rule it had been annexed to become part of the Russian empire in the 1860s. 'Russian Poland, Congress Poland', Engels stated in this preface, 'has become the big industrial region of the Russian Empire' (p. 114). Outside Poland, large-scale industry, he elaborated, was spread around a few parts of Russia, which was still a largely agricultural country with a mass peasantry. In the relatively small Polish territory, by way of contrast, industry was concentrated, and this resulted in both advantages and disadvantages. The advantages were the result of industry being economical in terms of production costs. A strange situation developed whereby, although Poland was now part of Russia, the competing Russian manufacturers acknowledged the advantages by demanding protective tariffs against Polish imports. The disadvantages, Engels went on, were for the Polish manufacturers and Russian government. The index then came back into the picture as he explained why this was so. The disadvantages were 'manifest in the rapid spread of socialist ideas among the Polish workers and in the growing demand for the Manifesto' (p. 114).

In the final paragraph of this preface Engels turned to the international context and significance of these developments in Poland. To grasp Engels' point in this preface it is necessary to recall a line of reasoning that Marx had made towards the end of the first main section of the *Manifesto*. Although the class struggle would ultimately be international, the proletariat would need initially to focus their efforts at the national level. The revolution would need to target the political systems and institutions of their respective countries which defended the bourgeoisie and subsequently international capital. When he said that Russian industry was being outstripped by that of Poland, thus illustrating the vitality of the Polish people and their ability to flourish as an independent nation, Engels was thus citing Poland as an example that helped substantiate the point Marx had made. Predicting that independence would soon be achieved, Engels suggested that it would be good not just for the Poles but also for the broader workers' movement. This was because the independence of each European nation was required for all these nations to achieve international collaboration.

Such independence had, Engels continued, already been gained for countries such as Germany, Italy and Hungary in the years since the uprisings of 1848, in which the revolutionary activity of the proletariat had actually helped consolidate the power of the bourgeoisie. In Poland in the 1860s, however, the Russian seizure of any remaining power the kingdom had until then retained meant that the nobility of the incorporated territory could not maintain such independence. The bourgeoisie that had come to dominate industry in the territory had, indeed, no interest in independence. So it was now the task of the Polish proletariat to engage in the struggle for independence. 'For the workers of all Europe', Engels suggested at the end of this preface, 'need the independence of Poland just as much as the Polish workers themselves' (p. 114). Having thus applied some of the theories of the 1848 *Manifesto* to Poland in the 1890s, he would similarly apply them to Germany and Italy in that decade in the last of the prefaces which traditionally appear in the various editions of the pamphlet.

Preface to the Italian edition of 1893

As was discussed in the first chapter of this guide, the *Manifesto* was conceived by Engels and Marx at the time of significant political unrest in a number of European countries. Just as the pamphlet went to press, this unrest had culminated in a series of uprisings in a number of cities on the continent. At the start of the preface to the Italian edition of 1893 Engels recalled that this had been the case and mentioned specifically those that had taken place in Milan and Berlin. As he noted, Italy and Germany had at that time been dominated by Austria and Russia, respectively. The armed uprisings of 1848, however, had helped bring the bourgeoisie to power, which in turn brought about the campaigns that were eventually successful for independence – independence being necessary for the bourgeoisie to operate as the ruling class.

As Engels noted, the armed uprising in Paris of 1848, while being unique in having the definite intention to overthrow the bourgeois regime, failed to achieve this objective. His brief analytical comment on the reasons for such failure in France not only offered a concise statement of the materialist conception of history, but also is significant because it indicates that Engels now knew that the 1848 revolutions had happened too early. The workers in France were, he claimed, conscious of the fatal antagonism that existed between their own class and the bourgeoisie. The problem was, he went on, that 'neither the economic progress of the country nor the intellectual development of the mass of French workers had as yet reached the stage which would have made a social reconstruction possible' (p. 115). This is an important statement. It represents recognition by Engels that this event in 1848 was an example of the sort of result he and Marx had expected when revolutionary change is attempted too early. The attempt had taken place before the structural and indeed superstructural conditions, driven by productive forces, had reached the stage at which the capitalist mode of production had become outdated.

Engels nevertheless also suggested that while the revolutions that coincided with the publication of the *Manifesto* had either brought the bourgeoisie to power (by which he meant political power) or consolidated such power, they had brought some progress. 'Thus', he suggested, 'if the Revolution of 1848 was not a socialist revolution, it paved the way, prepared the ground for the latter' (p. 115).

'Through the impetus given to large-scaled industry in all countries', Engels continued, 'the bourgeois regime during the last forty-five years has everywhere created a numerous, concentrated and powerful proletariat' (p. 115). This statement expressed very clearly a key aspect of the materialist conception of history. It conveyed the point that the capitalist system had fostered the growing power of the productive forces and thus required more workers to be gathered together to utilize those forces – forces which included their own exploited labour. This enabled those workers to enhance their power because of the consciousness and organizational abilities that such concentration fostered. The consciousness, moreover, would include recognition that the productive forces could be utilized to create an abundance of goods, thus causing the capitalist mode of production which relied upon scarcity to become outdated. Referring back to one of the most memorable phrases of the pamphlet, he said that the bourgeois regime 'has thus raised, to use the language of the Manifesto, its own grave-diggers' (p. 115).

Engels went on in this preface to restate the point he had made in the Polish edition the previous year that each nation would need to be autonomous and unified in order for the proletariat to take control in each country. Only then could the international system of cooperating workers' states work effectively for their common aims. The point he was making quite concisely and powerfully is, however, followed by one that, bearing the materialist conception in mind, raises a significant issue: 'Just imagine joint international action by the Italian, Hungarian, German, Polish and Russian workers under the political conditions preceding 1848!' The issue this raises is that of whether the political conditions were sufficient for such international collaboration and action given that the economic conditions had been relatively undeveloped in these countries in 1848. He believed that while political conditions had at that time been insufficient for such collaboration, the prospects for it were improving.

'The battles fought in 1848 were thus', Engels went on in the next paragraph, 'not fought in vain' (p. 116). He made a final and this time very brief statement evoking the materialist conception of history as follows: 'The fruits are ripening' (p. 116). In other words, the productive forces were reaching the stage of development at which industry would be so powerful as to create an abundance of goods. Were this to happen proletarian consciousness would develop, subsequently leading to political conditions that would be suitable for revolution.

Engels closed this preface – the last of those traditionally published with the *Manifesto* – by mentioning the Italian poet Dante very briefly. Of course, this being a preface to an Italian edition one can understand his reason. Making reference to this great figure of Italian literature was likely to appeal to the readership. Dante had been 'both the last poet of the Middle Ages and the first poet of modern times' (p. 116). Engels expressed hope that the beginning of the approaching new proletarian era would bring a new Dante to the scene. He nevertheless expressed such hope in the form of a question: 'Will Italy give us the new Dante, who will mark the hour of birth of this new proletarian era?' (p. 116) Most people today would judge that Italy and indeed the world have yet to witness either the new proletarian era or the accompanying new Dante. As will be seen in the next chapter, however, the reception of the *Manifesto* in Russia in the early twentieth century led to a revolution that persuaded many for the next several decades that such an era was in fact beginning.

Study questions

1 Why did Marx and Engels say in the preface to the 1872 German edition that no special stress should now be placed on the revolutionary measures that had been proposed at the end of Section II of the *Manifesto*?

2 Why did Marx and Engels suggest in the preface to the Russian edition of 1882 that the situations in Russia and the United States were changing significantly?

3 Why is the brief summary of Marx's 'basic thought' that Engels offered in the preface to the German edition of 1883 very useful to readers?

4 Why, according to Engels in the preface to the English edition of 1888, did an English trade union leader say that continental socialism had lost its terror?

5 Why did Engels say in the preface to the German edition of 1890 that the International Working Men's Association, which was by then extinct, was still having an influence on politics?

6 On what grounds did Engels express optimism in the preface to the Polish edition of 1892 that fundamental political change was forthcoming in that country?

7 Why did Engels express the view in the preface to the Italian edition of 1893 that the failed revolutions of 1848 had not been in vain?

CHAPTER FOUR

Reception and influence

This chapter provides a sketch of the some of the ways in which the *Manifesto* has been received since it appeared in 1848, along with some examples of its influence. It is indeed a sketch, and thus is by no means comprehensive. Nevertheless, hopefully it will stimulate interest among readers. Those who wish to research this reception and influence in further detail might turn to some of the books mentioned in the next chapter, which offers a guide to further reading. In this chapter the reception in the nineteenth century will be considered first, after we have turned very briefly to Russia.

As will be discussed in a little more detail later in this chapter, the revolutionary events in early-twentieth-century Russia, mentioned at the end of the previous chapter, brought about the greatest proliferation of both the publication and readership of the *Manifesto*. This development was not, however, restricted to Russia or indeed its post-revolutionary replacement the Soviet Union. Affordable editions of the pamphlet, for example, reached many English-reading socialists and communists in the twentieth century. Library copies were, moreover, frequently borrowed by academics and students around the world who were interested in the history of political thought. What may be surprising is that the huge readership that the *Manifesto* thus received stands in stark contrast to the period immediately after its publication early in 1848.

Europe in the nineteenth century

Readers may have noticed a 24-year gap between the publication of the first edition and that of 1872, the preface of which has come traditionally to be the first of the selection included in editions of the *Manifesto*. This reflects the fact that, after the original flurry of interest, the pamphlet did not have the influence that its authors hoped for. Although, as Marx and Engels boasted in the 1872 Preface, a number of editions had been published in the meantime, in reality, the readership had not been extensive and the impact of the pamphlet was thus limited. Even Macfarlane's English translation which, as Engels announced boldly (p. 106), appeared in the *Red Republican* newspaper, actually only reached a small audience and had very little influence.[1]

The 1848 uprisings were quelled and in the months that followed Marx himself lost interest in the League, in proletarian uprising and thus in the *Manifesto*. The revolutionary moment seemed to have passed and he returned to his journalistic activities to promote action that he hoped would bring about the sort of bourgeois republic that, eventually, could generate the conditions for proletarian revolution. Although he once again changed his mind the following year and began to revive his interest in the revolutionary course, the momentum could not be restored.[2]

Such little momentum as there was in the first few years after publication decreased still further when the Prussian police hunted down Communist League members, leading to the Cologne Communist Trial of 1852 at which a number were imprisoned. As was mentioned earlier in this guide, Engels would suggest in the Preface to an English edition 36 years later that the *Manifesto* 'seemed henceforth doomed to oblivion' (p. 107). Indeed, as Gareth Stedman Jones has put it: 'Between 1850 and 1870 the *Manifesto* was remembered by no more than a few hundred German-speaking veterans of the 1848 revolutions'.[3]

In the 1872 Preface, Marx and Engels expressed the belief that the *Manifesto* had by then become rather outdated. It was, in fact, chance, rather than forward planning that led to a revival of interest. The German authorities had searched the pamphlet for evidence in the trial that year of the leading social democrats August Bebel and Wilhelm Liebknecht. The authorities were determined to provide support for the charges of secret and dangerous subversive conspiracy. Liebknecht had been a member of the Communist League. This meant that the *Manifesto* as, of course, a pamphlet of that organization, could be used against him. Especially useful for this purpose was the declaration within the pamphlet that the working men had no country – evidence, perhaps, that they considered themselves opponents of the German state.

One consequence of the campaign by the German authorities against communism was the lifting of censorship. This facilitated publication of the new edition, which in turn brought about renewed interest, especially as there was a proliferation of left-leaning parties in many countries.[4] Nevertheless, such potential was not really fulfilled. While, indeed, the new situation meant there was a vast potential readership it would be a mistake to envisage masses of ordinary members of these parties rushing out in droves in response to the availability to buy copies of the pamphlet. The many editions across several countries were usually printed in relatively small numbers. Even this had required a rather unique occasion in order to stir significant interest. By way of coincidence, this occasion had materialized the previous year.

The event of 1871 which helped stimulate the interest that coincided with the lifting of censorship actually involved a new example of working-class activism. This event had in turn been brought about by the Prussian army's siege of Paris. At the end of the Franco-Prussian War of 1870–71, before the defeated French authorities had colluded with the invading forces to allow the brutal invasion of the city in which many thousands of Parisians were slaughtered, the surrounded citizens formed new structures of government. In his public address *The Civil War in France*, which was published as a pamphlet, Marx offered a detailed account of these structures that, he hoped, would provide an example for a post-revolutionary society. In his private correspondence Marx was quite critical of the actions of the Parisian Communards as he was not optimistic that they would be successful. One can thus perhaps appreciate why, in the published address, he was decidedly measured in his analysis, being fully aware that the Commune was not infallible and certainly not a ready-made utopia. He knew that it was not an unambiguously communist or socialist arrangement. Such an arrangement would have needed a far greater process of transformation[5] Nevertheless, this example of working people taking government into their own hands, along with his public support for it, rekindled interest in the *Manifesto* just before, as we have seen, it was about to become available once again. It is in this climate that Engels declared in the 1888 English edition that there had been many new editions published in a range of languages (pp. 107–108). As mentioned earlier, he said in that Preface that the *Manifesto* had 'come to the front again' (p. 107).

'To the front' is indeed quite an accurate statement if we are to interpret those words as avante garde. It was among those of the avante garde, rather than throughout the movement, that the pamphlet made an impact. While Marx, as we have seen, began to align himself with relatively moderate trade unionists within the workers' movement, it was the committed activists rather than lay-members who tended to read the pamphlet.[6] Furthermore, as Isaac suggests, the text itself now had a new life, losing its status as a party document as Engels changed its name from *Manifesto of the Communist Party* to simply the *Communist Manifesto*.[7] Thus, the revived *Manifesto* was portrayed and perceived in a rather different way than had been the case originally. Rather than as primarily a pamphlet or indeed a manifesto it was now often considered, as Stedman Jones comments, to be part of a broader project of the materialist conception of history.[8]

Stedman Jones suggests that this process of transformation had actually begun when Engels initiated this new way of interpreting the *Manifesto* in the late 1850s. This, according to Stedman Jones, was with collusion on the part of Marx. Engels had begun to present his and Marx's ideas as though they were contributions to a new scientific discovery.[9] Engels did indeed play such a role in the nurturing of a Marxist ideology, not least in the essay 'Karl Marx' he wrote in 1877. Marx's name was now, Engels claimed in that essay, 'inscribed in the annals of science' first for revolutionizing 'the whole conception of world history' and second for discovering and elucidating 'the relation between capital and labour'.[10] Marx himself was, nevertheless, doing more than just collude in this respect. As we have seen at a number of points in this guide, he suggested in the 'Preface to *A Critique of Political Economy*' in 1859 that the *Manifesto* was one of a series of works through which his guiding thread ran. Marx was thus himself playing a major role in the transformation of the *Manifesto*.

Notwithstanding the tendency for only committed activists to actually read its full text in the late nineteenth century, the change in the status of the *Manifesto* to one component of a complex and scientific system made it suitable for a major revival of a particular sort early in the century that followed. In fact, 'revival' is an understatement because, as mentioned earlier, it reached a readership far greater than at any previous time. This began to happen when the Russian Marxists got their hands on it. The *Communist Manifesto* would become a key text for those in the vanguard of the revolution and subsequently for the activists who subscribed to the ideological position of Marxism-Leninism.

The Bolsheviks and communism in the twentieth century

The Marxist who did most to bring about the revival of the *Manifesto* in Russia was Lenin. In the early years of the twentieth century, he worked as a wily political operator to reshape the Russian Social Democratic and Labour Party, splitting his supporters (Bolsheviks) from the rest (Mensheviks) in 1903. His group would go on to become the Communist Party. Lenin's most widely read works included *What Is to Be Done?*, *Imperialism, the Highest Stage of Capitalism* and *The State and Revolution*. In these writings he produced the most influential Marxist theories of the entire century. *What Is to Be Done?* was a pamphlet on the revolutionary organization of the proletariat as a vanguard, itself led by a higher vanguard of professional revolutionaries. *Imperialism* offered a discussion of international capitalism and what Lenin saw as the likelihood of its demise. It is in the third of these works – *The State and Revolution* – that the significance of the *Manifesto* is most prominent.[11]

In *The State and Revolution* Lenin once again took up the notion of professional revolutionaries who were educated by Marxism. Such education produced a workers' party that would take the role of 'the vanguard of the proletariat, capable of assuming power and leading the whole people to socialism, of directing and organising the new system, of being the teacher, the guide, the leader of all the working and exploited people'.[12] As discussed later, the party would also have a rather less benign role in its relations with the bourgeoisie.

Lenin manipulated the text of the *Manifesto* in order to tie it to his own interpretation of the concept of dictatorship of the proletariat which Marx had employed in some of his other writings. Marx had first used this concept in *The Class Struggles in France*, two years after the publication of the *Manifesto*. He also mentioned it very briefly in his letter to Weydemeyer in 1852 and the 'Critique of the Gotha Programme' in 1875. He did not make altogether clear in these writings what he meant by dictatorship. It is perhaps significant, however, that the term tended to be associated in the nineteenth century with the granting of supreme power to a ruler in ancient Rome for six months for the purpose of defending the republic.[13] Marx employed the term accordingly to signify a transitional period of rule by the proletariat, which is consistent with the temporary nature of dictatorship as it was commonly understood.

Commenting on Marx and Engels' argument in the *Manifesto* that the proletariat should organize as a ruling class, and thus form a kind of state, Lenin suggested not unreasonably in *The State and Revolution* that this can be seen as a formulation of the dictatorship of the proletariat.[14] Although Marx did not actually use the term dictatorship of the proletariat in the *Manifesto*, there does seem to be some consistency between this important point in it on the one hand and the customary nineteenth-century usage of the term on the other hand.

Lenin went on in *The State and Revolution* to build on Marx's use of the term in a manner that implies a meaning closer to that which is usually associated with 'dictatorship' today: that of autocratic or authoritarian rule. Marx's application of the theory of class struggle to the question of the state and revolution led, according to Lenin, 'as a matter of course to the recognition of the political rule of the proletariat, of its dictatorship, i.e., of undivided power directly backed by armed force of the people'. The proletariat, formed as the new ruling class, would need, if it really wanted to overthrow the old system, to be 'capable of crushing the inevitable and desperate resistance' of the bourgeoisie.[15]

Marx's use of the term 'despotic' (p. 91) in his assessment of the measures the proletarian state would need to undertake to replace the capitalist social order may give the impression that he would have concurred with Lenin's interpretation. We cannot know for certain whether or not that would have been so. Turning, however, to the regime that Stalin built after the power struggle in the Soviet Union following the death of Lenin, one does find that Marx's ideas, and moreover those of Lenin, were manipulated very grossly.

When Stalin assumed the leadership of the Soviet Union in the 1920s, the crucial internationalist element of the *Manifesto*—an element that, as we have seen, became particularly prominent in the prefaces of the 1870s, 1880s and 1890s—was downplayed. In formulating and implementing the doctrine of 'socialism in one country', Stalin demoted international revolution to a long-term goal.[16] Lenin's co-leader of the revolution Leon Trotsky insisted, as have many of his followers since, that the abandonment of such a key element was the reason why Stalin's regime became a degenerate workers' state rather than the communist society for which, Marx had hoped, international revolution would pave the way.[17] The system of government and suppression that Stalin set up and maintained for a quarter of a century was archetypal of the sort of brutal regime we now categorize as a dictatorship. Trotsky argued that the nature of Stalin's Soviet Union was 'a deadly illustration of the falsehood of the theory of socialism in one country'. This was a theory, Trotsky insisted, that was based on an attempt to liquidate the key message of the *Manifesto* that the 'international development of capitalism implies the international character of the proletarian revolution'.[18]

Nevertheless, degenerate and brutal as Stalin's treatment of Marxism was, the distant goal of worldwide revolution helped inspire an international communist movement emanating from, and loyal to, Moscow. This movement would ensure the *Manifesto* would be made available for readers in many different countries for much of the century until the sudden demise of Soviet communism from 1989 to 1991.[19] English-language editions of Marx and Engels' *Selected Works*, for example, were published by the communist-affiliated Lawrence and Wishart, having been prepared in Moscow first by the Marx–Engels–Lenin Institute in the 1940s and again by Progress Publishers in the 1968.[20] In communist China, furthermore, inexpensive English-language copies of the *Manifesto* and many other works by Marx and Engels were published for distribution around the world, including Western countries in which capitalism was developing at a rapid pace.

The Soviet Union and Chinese communist regimes were thus influential in propagating the message of the *Manifesto* in other countries that, with their developed capitalist economies, Marx and Engels might have said were more suitable for communist revolution. So too was the Trotskyite movement that, as mentioned earlier, challenged the Stalinist interpretation of Marxism and Leninism. Nevertheless, as was illustrated by Harold Laski's centenary edition of the pamphlet, published with his substantial Introduction, interest in the *Manifesto* extended beyond the rival movements fighting to assume the Leninist mantle.

The west in the twentieth century

Laski was a prominent member of the Labour Left who sympathized with much of Marx's theory but insisted upon the democratic, parliamentary road to socialism. The Foreword contributed by the British Labour Party in 1948 to Laski's edition of the *Manifesto* acknowledged 'the indebtedness to Marx and Engels as two of the men who have been the inspiration of the whole working-class movement'.[21] Thereafter, however, Labour entered a long period in which it would have been increasingly unlikely to find such an acknowledgement offered on behalf of the party. From the perspective of the second decade of the twenty-first century, it seems that the days when the Party would have made such a declaration are long gone. In fact, even at its most radical, the Marxism to which Labour's ideology in the early to mid-twentieth century bore closest resemblance was that of the German social democrat Eduard Bernstein.

Bernstein's revisionist Marxism, first published in the very last year of the nineteenth century, rejected the dialectics and revolutionary elements of the ideology.[22] Adherents to the theories that the collapse of the bourgeois economy was imminent, and that radical social democracy could and should be induced by this prospect, were, he declared, wrong. Moreover, they were mistaken, he insisted, to base this theory on the conclusions of the *Communist Manifesto*. The *Manifesto* was, Bernstein suggested, correct in so far as it characterized the general tendencies of the evolution of modern society. Marx and Engels' pamphlet was, however, mistaken 'in the estimate of the time the evolution would take'.[23]

It was likely to take far longer than they had surmised when they drafted and wrote the *Manifesto* in 1847–8 and it would probably take a form not at all like that which they had foreseen. The class structure of modern industrialized societies was now very different from that of the mid-nineteenth century. The working class, moreover, was now able to achieve gradual reforms of capitalism. Marx and Engels had themselves in their later work recognized such changes.

Bernstein's point about different timescales and different forms of evolution reflected the preference of many among the European working classes for reform rather than revolution. The class polarization that Marx predicted in the *Manifesto* did not, furthermore, materialize. Bernstein's identification of a growing middle class was, indeed, more accurate. For these reasons Bernstein's analysis of the *Manifesto* has remained pertinent.

Nevertheless, subscribers to various interpretations of Marxism and even many non-Marxists have continued throughout the twentieth and early twenty-first centuries to insist that revisionism went too far. Relations between the proletariat on the one side and the bourgeoisie with the state as its political executive on the other can, they argue, be interpreted in terms of class conflict. In more severe examples such as the coup against the Marxist-leaning President Allende in Chile in 1973 this conflict has involved overt deadly force. In other, far less extreme examples, the state in capitalist democracies has through legislation, privatization, reduction of expenditure, employment of the media and occasionally use of force helped secure the interests of the bourgeoisie.[24] The international aspect of the world portrayed in the *Manifesto* can, moreover, be perceived in the operations of multinational corporations that are allowed and even enabled by states to exploit workers of their countries.

The twenty-first century

The international aspect of capitalism that Marx anticipated in the first main section of the *Manifesto* has been expanded and intensified in recent decades in processes driven by the forces of globalization. This was the context of the demonstration in 1999 at the meeting of the World Trade Organization in Seattle and the response of the police. The violent clashes have been dubbed the 'Battle in Seattle'. A worldwide movement was soon beginning to develop surrounding the World Social Forum that was formed to counter the World Economic Forum of international capitalism. Continuing into the twenty-first century, these processes rekindled interest in the *Manifesto* as many radical activists and writers began to participate in the anti-capitalist movement. In this climate in 2003, Alex Callinicos offered his *Anti-Capitalist Manifesto* for which, he declared, Marx and Engels' *Manifesto* was a major reference point. The broader movement was, he added, inspired by Marx and Engels' critique of the capitalist mode of production 'in both theory and practice, even if most of its activists would reject the label "Marxist"'.[25] In his view, anti-capitalism was necessary because 'the processes of proletarianization that Marx and Engels portrayed in the *Communist Manifesto* continue on a world scale'.[26] One reason why this is significant is that it indicates that the *Communist Manifesto* had by now become so influential that its tenets and arguments had permeated the intellectual and political environment to the extent that they were no longer necessarily associated with their authors.

Among other intellectuals involved in the contemporary anti-capitalist movement were Michael Hardt and Antonio Negri. In their book *Empire* published in 2000, they used the term 'imperialism' to describe the extension of the sovereignty of European states to territories beyond their formal boundaries. They acknowledged that sovereignty in its traditional state form which could extend in such a way had declined, but argued that a new form had emerged, which they called 'Empire'. This global form of sovereignty was 'composed of a series of national and supranational organisms united under a single logic of rule'.[27] They hoped their book would contribute 'a general theoretical framework and a toolbox of concepts for theorizing and acting in and against Empire'.[28] While at almost 500 pages in length, *Empire* was, of course, many times longer than Marx and Engels' concise *Manifesto*, one can thus see that Hardt and Negri were likewise presenting a work that combined political philosophy with a manifesto for action.

Hardt and Negri referred to Marx and Engels' pamphlet as a 'paradigmatic political manifesto'. They argued, nevertheless, that it was now outdated in the age of Empire. Attempts to apply the message of the *Manifesto* over 150 years after it had been written would be unsuccessful because its narrative was essentially a self-constituting collective action aimed at its objective. The growing organization of the modern proletariat, its authors had assumed, directly entailed the creation of the Communist party or of communism as a movement. The global nature of capitalism today meant that all the powers of humanity contributed to the ways that labour, society and life itself were now being reproduced. Politics had in this environment become far less transparent than it had been before the global era as the relationships by which power and control were imposed upon society and life were now hidden. The workers could no longer find the means of their liberation in such an organized movement against a clear target.[29]

In a later article, Hardt and Negri reiterated that the opposition to this contemporary form of capitalism and its politics cannot be the same as the old proletarian struggles that Marx had advocated. They elaborated on the portrayal that Marx had once offered of the situation in terms of a burrowing mole. The mole, Hardt and Negri imagined, could be seen to be digging a network of tunnels that linked various uprisings and campaigns together. Marx, they suggested, was implying that when one such struggle failed, its tactics contributed to the broader struggle that would eventually bring the capitalist order down. Hardt and Negri argued that the mole metaphor was no longer appropriate, given that the nature of Empire meant that the old approach of interconnected struggles was now outdated. A more appropriate metaphor was that of a snake slithering around the world without the methodical purpose of Marx's mole. The strengths of each of the struggles against capitalism lay in their relative isolation from other such struggles against the common enemy which is Empire. Each struggle could use all its strength to recoil and strike, rather than wait for coordination or direction from a broader movement.[30]

While Hardt and Negri thus implied rather than directly stated that their book was an attempt to take the place of Marx and Engels' 'paradigmatic' pamphlet, the Marxist writer Slavoj Žižek has been more direct. Žižek has suggested clearly that the aim of the authors of *Empire* was to offer a new version of the *Manifesto* suitable for the very different situation of twenty-first-century global capitalism.[31] He thus interpreted *Empire* as the equivalent of the *Manifesto* for the contemporary period of globalization. Žižek found much with which he could agree in Hardt and Negri's thesis that the global triumph of capitalism permeates all aspects of the lives of people the world over, while leaving behind its old territorial basis, thus making the capitalist system more vulnerable. The 'fundamental corrosion of all important social connections', he concurred, 'lets the genie out of the bottle: it sets free the potentially centrifugal forces that the capitalist system is no longer fully able to control'. Capitalism, he went on, paraphrasing a famous line in the *Manifesto*, 'digs its own grave'.[32] Nevertheless, in comparing Marx and Engels' pamphlet with this new 'manifesto', he considers the latter unfavourably. The problem with Hardt and Negri's thesis, he insisted, was that it was 'pre-Marxist', by which he meant that it failed to identify one of the key themes of the *Manifesto*. Hardt and Negri's *Empire* does not, according to Žižek, deal with the question of how, and indeed whether the global, socioeconomic process of the present time will create the space needed for the radical measures that will bring down the capitalist system. Hardt and Negri, he elaborated, 'fail to repeat, in today's conditions, Marx's line of argumentation which held that the prospect of the proletarian revolution emerges out of the inherent antagonisms of the capitalist mode of production'.[33]

We have now reached the point where we are considering how a new manifesto is being received by a prominent Marxist critic who is concerned with whether or not its authors are successful in their aspiration to play the role of Marx and Engels today. This perhaps illustrates just how significant and resonant the *Manifesto* really is in the history of political thought. It serves as a starting point in the assessment of critical analyses of the international capitalist system. Newer theories are judged in part on the basis of whether they can improve on this work of 1848.

The present study of Marx and Engels' famous pamphlet, of the prefaces written later and appended to it, and of the reception it has received over a period of more than 16 decades since it was published, helps show that some of its basic assumptions have required qualification. Social, economic and political developments have not always turned out in the ways the authors expected.[34] Nevertheless, the continuing prominence of the *Manifesto* indicates that Townshend is on firm ground when he makes the following prediction: 'As long as capitalism remains in business, Marxism as a movement and doctrine, in whatever form, is likely to remain obstinately relevant'.[35] Readers who concur with this judgement might peruse the final chapter of this guide for advice on further reading.

CHAPTER FIVE

Further reading

The Communist Manifesto

The version of the *Manifesto* used most extensively in this guide is edited and introduced by Jeffrey C. Isaac. Published in 2012 in the Yale University Press *Rethinking the Western Tradition* series, it is easily accessible at a reasonable cost. It also includes essays on the *Manifesto* and Marxism by several well-known authorities in the field. The page numbers of this edition, rather than the slightly more recent second edition of the version edited by Frederic L. Bender, have been referenced in brackets in the text of this guide. Bender's version has, nevertheless, been referenced at several points in this guide. The Isaac version has been chosen for two main reasons. First, while, like Bender's, it includes the full range of prefaces that have traditionally accompanied the *Manifesto* – the earlier ones written by Marx and Engels and the later ones by Engels alone, after the death of Marx – Isaac places them after the main text rather than before. This encourages readers to turn initially to the main text and then its prefaces chronologically in the order in which they were written. Second, and very importantly, readers are encouraged to use the Isaac version because it includes the two drafts written by Engels, which Marx drew on when he wrote the *Manifesto*.

Like the other editions of the *Manifesto* mentioned in this chapter, except for the one translated by Terrell Carver for his selection *Marx: Later Political Writings*, Isaac's edition presents

Moore's translation of 1888, which Engels helped prepare for publication. As readers of the present guide will have found, Carver's translation is actually very useful in that in a few cases it helps clarify the point of sentences that are less clear in the Moore translation.

Like that of Isaac, Bender's version is easily accessible and reasonably priced. Published in 2013 in the *Norton Critical Editions* series, it includes informative introductory material and a selection of readings from the literature about the *Manifesto*. Unusually, this edition cites Marx alone as the author, rather than Marx and Engels. This is not unreasonable considering that, as mentioned earlier, Marx was the author of the main text of the pamphlet. Nevertheless, given Engels' contribution, it is also very reasonable to name him along with Marx, as do most other editions.

There have been many other English-language editions of the *Manifesto*. Just a few will be mentioned here: some of the more recent and accessible ones, two classic ones and an online edition. Of the recent editions, a useful, basic one is number 13 of the *Penguin Great Ideas* series. Lacking an editorial introduction and printed without the various prefaces, it, nevertheless, gives readers who read the pamphlet and wish to explore more of Marx's work a taste in the form of sections of 'The Eighteenth Brumaire of Louis Bonaparte'. In the latter work, Marx was concerned with political events surrounding the coup d'état of Napoleon III in France in 1851. Although appearing to rule autonomously, this self-styled emperor relied on the support of the peasants and had to serve capitalist interests in order to maintain power. Marx also indicated that the conditions for proletarian revolution were developing beneath the surface. This selection includes the passage mentioned by Hardt and Negri (discussed in the previous chapter of this guide) where Marx portrays the channels of this development in terms of a burrowing mole.

Also published by Penguin was an edition of the *Manifesto* with a substantial and very informative introduction by Gareth Stedman Jones. At almost 200 pages in length, Stedman Jones's introduction is the equivalent of a book on the context and reception of the *Manifesto*, on the contributions of the two authors and on the lasting influence the pamphlet has had. This edition also contains the full traditional range of prefaces, as does the *Oxford*

World Classics edition, which has a clear and concise introduction by David McLellan. The latter introduction mainly discusses the political and intellectual environment in which the pamphlet was produced.

Another useful, recent edition of the *Manifesto* is published by Verso with an introduction by Eric Hobsbawm. He discusses the context and reception and goes on to discuss both strengths and weaknesses of the pamphlet. As he suggests, although in many ways it became outdated, it has continuing significance in its discussion of the early stages of what would later become known as globalized capitalism. This edition, however, includes only Engels' preface to the English edition of 1888, rather than the full range of prefaces.

Many authors of introductions to the *Manifesto* have offered interpretations that vary in approach, stance and style. In addition to those just mentioned, interested readers may wish to search libraries for others, including those of two very prominent twentieth-century intellectuals: Harold Laski and A.J. P. Taylor. Laski's *Communist Manifesto: Socialist Landmark*, mentioned in the previous chapter of this guide, was published in the centenary year of the *Manifesto* in 1948. It consisted of a substantial introduction by Laski, followed by the entire text of the pamphlet along with most of the traditionally appended prefaces (but not those to the Polish edition of 1892 or the Italian edition of 1893). In his introduction Laski emphasized ways in which the *Manifesto* remained resonant in 1948. By way of contrast, in an introduction to an edition published 19 years later, Taylor criticized what he considered to be the shortcomings of Marx's analysis in the *Manifesto*. These shortcomings, according to Taylor, included Marx's tendency to generalize on the basis of insufficient evidence, his presentation of a false picture of the working class and his simplistic view of class and industrial relations in the modern society.

The *Manifesto* is also included in McLellan's edited *Karl Marx: Selected Writings*. This version includes McLellan's brief but informative introduction to the pamphlet. Note, however, that a number of the prefaces to the pamphlet are not included in this volume. The two prefaces that are included appear later in the book, as the selected writings are presented in chronological order.

Editions of the Manifesto

Karl Marx and Friedrich Engels, *The Communist Manifesto*, edited by Jeffrey C. Isaac. New Haven and London: Yale University Press, 2012.
Karl Marx, *The Communist Manifesto*, edited by Frederic L. Bender. New York and London: WW Norton and Company, 2013.
Karl Marx and Friedrich Engels, *The Communist Manifesto*, with an introduction by Gareth Stedman Jones. London: Penguin 2002.
Karl Marx and Engels, Friedrich Engels, *The Communist Manifesto*. London: Penguin Books – Great Ideas, 2004.
Karl Marx and Friedrich Engels, *The Communist Manifesto*, with an introduction by David McLellan. Oxford: Oxford University Press, 1998.
Karl Marx and Frederick Engels (2012), *The Communist Manifesto*, with an introduction by Eric Hobsbawm. London: Verso, 2012.
Karl Marx and Friedrich Engels, *The Communist Manifesto*, with an introduction by A. J. P. Taylor. Harmondsworth: Penguin, 1967.
Harold J. Laski, *Communist Manifesto: Socialist Landmark*. London: George Allen and Unwin, 1948.
Karl Marx and Friedrich Engels, 'The Communist Manifesto', in David McLellan (ed.), *Karl Marx: Selected Writings*. Oxford: Oxford University Press, 2000.
Karl Marx and Friedrich Engels, 'Manifesto of the Communist Party', in Terrell Carver (ed. and trans.), *Marx: Later Political Writings*. Cambridge: Cambridge University Press, 1996.
Karl Marx and Frederick Engels, 'Manifesto of the Communist Party', in Karl Marx and Frederick Engels, *Selected Works in One Volume*. London: Lawrence and Wishart, 1968.

Selected works and collected works

McLellan's very useful selection of Marx's writings is available at a reasonable price and can also be found in many libraries. Divided into chronological sections, the book includes McLellan's own very useful commentaries both at the beginning of the sections and before each of the selected works. As mentioned earlier, it does include the *Manifesto* (but without the prefaces) and a few other pieces written jointly by Marx and Engels, but not anything written independently by Engels.

An exceptional and easily accessible online source is the *Marxists Internet Archive*, which can be found at http://www.marxists.org/index.htm. While it does not hold a comprehensive collection of the writings of Marx and Engels, the site does include many of their works including the Moore translation of the *Manifesto*. Indeed, readers may decide to use this as their first port of call when looking for particular items written by these authors.

Readers with access to libraries may be able to find Marx/Engels: *Selected Works in One Volume* and Karl Marx: *Selected Works in Two Volumes*, published by Lawrence and Wishart in 1968 and 1942, respectively. Very popular for a number of decades, these will still be very useful to readers today. Indeed, the *Selected Works in One Volume* has been referenced in the present guide in a number of cases where either items are not in McLellan's *Selected Writings* or where McLellan does not include the passage in his edited selection from the work in question.

Selections

David McLellan (ed.), *Karl Marx: Selected Writings*, second edition. Oxford: Oxford University Press, 2000.

Karl Marx and Frederick Engels, 'Marx and Engels Internet Archive' at http://www.marxists.org/archive/marx/works/sw/index.htm in *Marxists Internet Archive*: http://www.marxists.org/index.htm.

Karl Marx: *Selected Works in Two Volumes*. London: Lawrence and Wishart, 1942.

Karl Marx and Frederick Engels, *Selected Works in One Volume*. London: Lawrence and Wishart, 1968.

Some other books by Marx and Engels

In some cases this guide has discussed or mentioned works by Marx and/or Engels that are not available in the easily accessible printed selections. Reasonably inexpensive editions have been referenced in such cases.

Reasonably inexpensive editions of important works

Karl Marx, *Capital Volume One*. Harmondsworth: Penguin, 1976. [This edition includes a substantial Introduction by Ernest Mandel.]
Friedrich Engels, *The Condition of the Working Class in England*. Oxford: Oxford University Press, 1993.
Karl Marx and Frederick Engels, *The German Ideology*. London: Lawrence and Wishart, second edition, 1974. [This edition includes Part One and selections from Parts Two and Three.]

Biographies

For details of the life and works of Marx, McLellan's *Karl Marx: A Biography* has become the standard scholarly work. A more recent biography is Jonathan Sperber's *Karl Marx: A Nineteenth Century Life*. Sperber stresses that his is very much a study of Marx's life and ideas in the context of his own times. Readers who would prefer to start with a lighter, lively and in some places very amusing biography should select Francis Wheen's *Karl Marx*. A scholarly but easily readable biography of Engels is Tristram Hunt's *The Frock-Coated Communist*. While not formally a biography, Paul Thomas's useful short book *Karl Marx* focuses on Marx's life and considers his ideas against the background of that life.

Useful biographies

David McLellan, *Karl Marx: A Biography*, fourth edition. Basingstoke: Palgrave Macmillan, 2006.
Jonathan Sperber, *Karl Marx: a Nineteenth-Century Life*. New York: Liveright Publishing Corporation, 2013.
Francis Wheen, *Karl Marx*. London: Fourth Estate, 1999.
Tristram Hunt, *The Frock-Coated Communist: The Life and Times of the Original Champagne Socialist*. London: Penguin, 2010. (This was published in the USA as Tristram Hunt,

Marx's General: The Revolutionary Life of Friedrich Engels.
New York: Metropolitan Books, 2009.)
Paul Thomas, *Karl Marx*. London: Reaktion, 2012.

Basic introductions to Marx and Engels

There are many basic introductions to the work of Marx. There are less of such introductions to the work of Engels. This section lists just a few of those to each author. They are pitched at various levels. I have tried to indicate this rather loosely by placing the less demanding ones earlier. However, this is not precise and so the order of the list should certainly not be taken to be very exact.

Useful introductions

Gill Hands, *Marx: The Key Ideas*. London: Teach Yourself, Hodder, 2010.
Peter Osborne, *How to Read Marx*. London: Granta, 2005.
Andrew Collier, *Marx: A Beginner's Guide*. Oxford: Oneworld, 2004.
Peter Singer, *Marx: A Very Short Introduction*. Oxford: Oxford University Press, 2000.
Terrell Carver, *Engels: A Very Short Introduction*. Oxford: Oxford University Press, 2003.
David McLellan, *Engels*. Glasgow: Fontana/Collins, 1977.
David McLellan, *Marx*. Glasgow: Fontana/Collins, 1975.
John Seed, *Marx: A Guide for the Perplexed*. London: Continuum, 2010.
Jon Elster, *An Introduction to Karl Marx*. Cambridge: Cambridge University Press, 1986.

Other useful books on Marx and Engels

There are very many books that could have been listed in this section. Those that have been selected will be helpful to readers who are newcomers to Marx and Engels. Some are recent and others, while being older, are still valuable for the information they provide and the clarity with which they present it. I have included just a few of the many more difficult and advanced books. Readers who wish to continue their studies will be able to find many more such books, along with articles in academic and specialist journals, by following the references in those included here.

Among the books listed here is Terrell Carver's study of the intellectual relationship of Marx and Engels. This will be a particularly useful source for those seeking a fuller understanding of the ways in which the joint authors worked and collaborated. Readers who wish to find short accounts of key concepts, works, themes and people will find Ian Fraser and Lawrence Wilde's *The Marx Dictionary* very helpful. Jonathan Wolff's short book *Why Read Marx Today* offers a clear and concise account of his critique of capitalism.

Useful books on Marx and Engels

Terrell Carver, *Marx and Engels: The Intellectual Relationship*. Brighton: Wheatsheaf Books, 1983.
Ian Fraser and Lawrence Wilde, *The Marx Dictionary*. London: Continuum, 2011.
Jonathan Wolff, *Why Read Marx Today?* Oxford: Oxford University Press, 2002.
Alex Callinicos, *The Revolutionary Ideas of Karl Marx*, second edition. London: Bookmarks, 1996.
Terry Eagleton, *Why Marx Was Right*. New Haven: Yale University Press, 2011.
Terry Eagleton, *Marx*. London: Phoenix, 1997.
Jon Elster, *Making Sense of Marx*. Cambridge: Cambridge University Press, 1985.
David McLellan, *Marx before Marxism*, revised edition. Harmondsworth: Penguin, 1972.
Michael Evans, *Karl Marx*. London: George Allen and Unwin, 1975.
Mark Cowling and Lawrence Wilde (eds), *Approaches to Marx*. Milton Keynes: Open University Press, 1989.
Terrell Carver, *Marx's Social Theory*. Oxford: Oxford University Press, 1982.

Terrell Carver, *The Postmodern Marx*. Manchester: Manchester University Press, 1998.
Bhikhu Parekh, *Marx's Theory of Ideology*. London: Croom Helm, 1982.
Paul Thomas, *Karl Marx and the Anarchists*. London: Routledge and Kegan Paul, 1980.
G.A. Cohen, *Karl Marx's Theory of History: A Defence*. Oxford: Oxford University Press, 1978.
Norman Geras, *Marx and Human Nature: Refutation of a Legend*. London: Verso, 1983.
Ernst Fischer, *Marx in His Own Words*. Harmondsworth: Penguin, 1970.

Marxism

This section includes a selection of books that discuss the various intellectual, social and political movements that have either declared themselves to be Marxist or been profoundly influenced by the work of Marx and Engels. Some of these books are now quite old. Nevertheless, they provide useful details and are written in clear English suitable to readers beginning to learn about the ways in which the *Manifesto* has inspired many people since it first appeared in 1848.

The *Marxists Internet Archive* at http://www.marxists.org/index.htm includes works by many Marxists. For readers who intend to research the broader context of Marxism there are also relevant writings of non-Marxists in the archive. As is the case for works by Marx and Engels, readers may decide to use this web site as a first port of call when looking for writings by particular other authors.

Useful books on Marxism

Geoff Boucher, *Understanding Marxism*. Durham: Acumen Publishing, 2012.
Matthew Johnson (ed.), *The Legacy of Marxism*. London: Continuum, 2012.

David McLellan, *Marxism after Marx*, fourth edition. Basingstoke: Palgrave Macmillan, 2007.
Jonathan Joseph, *Marxism and Social Theory*. Basingstoke: Palgrave Macmillan, 2006.
Tom Bottomore (ed.), *A Dictionary of Marxist Thought*, second edition. Oxford: Blackwell, 1991.
Jules Townshend, *The Politics of Marxism: The Critical Debates*. London: Leicester University Press, 1996.
Bradley J. Macdonald, *Performing Marx: Contemporary Negotiations of a Living Tradition*. Albany: SUNY, 2006.
Alex Callinicos, *Marxism and Philosophy*. Oxford: Oxford University Press, 1985.
Joseph V. Femia, *Marxism and Democracy*. Oxford: Clarendon, 1993.
Betty Matthews (ed.), *Marx: 100 Years On*. London: Lawrence and Wishart, 1983.
Robin Blackburn (ed.), *Revolution and Class Struggle: A Reader in Marxist Politics*. Glasgow: Fontana/Collins, 1977.
C. Wright Mills, *The Marxists*. Harmondsworth: Penguin, 1963.
R.N. Carew Hunt, *The Theory and Practice of Communism*. Harmondsworth: Penguin, 1963.
Bertram D. Wolfe, *Marxism: 100 Years in the Life of a Doctrine*. London: Chapman and Hall, 1967.
Edmund Wilson, *To the Finland Station: A Study in the Writing and Acting of History*. London: Fontana, 1960.

Anti-capitalism

This final, short section includes just two of the most prominent books that contributed to the anti-capitalist literature of the early twenty-first century. Michael Hardt and Antonio Negri suggested that a new manifesto was needed now that Marx and Engels' original had become outdated. Alex Callinicos insisted on the continuing relevance of the *Communist Manifesto* which, he declared, influenced his own manifesto. This helps illustrate that Marx and Engels' *Manifesto* is of importance to some sections of the global anti-capitalist movement of the twenty-first century.

Two important books of contemporary anti-capitalism

Alex Callinicos, *An Anti-Capitalist Manifesto*. Cambridge: Polity, 2003.

Michael Hardt and Antonio Negri, *Empire*. Cambridge MA: Harvard University Press, 2000.

NOTES

Introduction

1 Norman Geras, 'What does it mean to be a Marxist?', in Matthew Johnson (ed.), *The Legacy of Marxism: Contemporary Challenges, Conflicts and Developments*. London: Continuum, 2012, pp. 13–23.

Chapter One

1 Alex Callinicos, *The Revolutionary Ideas of Karl Marx*, 2nd edn. London: Bookmarks, 1996, pp. 52–5.
2 John Seed, *Marx: A Guide for the Perplexed*. London: Continuum, 2010, p. 31.
3 Eric Hobsbawm, 'Introduction' in Karl Marx and Frederick Engels, *The Communist Manifesto*. London: Verso, 2012, pp. 4–5; Gareth Stedman Jones, Gareth (2002), Introduction' in Karl Marx and Friedrich Engels (eds), *The Communist Manifesto*. London: Penguin, 2002, pp. 14–15.
4 Frederic L. Bender, 'Historic and Theoretical Backgrounds of the *Communist Manifesto*' in Karl Marx (ed.), *The Communist Manifesto*. W. W. Norton and Company: New York and London, 2013, pp. 1–2.
5 Harold J. Laski, *Communist Manifesto: Socialist Landmark*. London: George Allen and Unwin, 1948.
6 Stedman Jones, 'Introduction', pp. 27–38.
7 Hobsbawm, 'Introduction', pp. 5–6.
8 Tristram Hunt, *The Frock-Coated Communist: The Life and Times of the Original Champagne Socialist*. London: Penguin, 2010, pp. 12–77.
9 Hunt, *Frock-Coated Communist*, pp. 78–117.

10 Friedrich Engels, *The Condition of the Working Class in England*. Oxford: Oxford University Press, 1993.
11 David McLellan, *Karl Marx: A Biography*, 4th edn. Basingstoke: Palgrave Macmillan, 2006, pp. 1–13.
12 Francis Wheen, *Karl Marx*. London: Fourth Estate, 1999, pp. 14–17; McLellan, *Karl Marx: A Biography*, pp. 13–15.
13 There is a useful Marx family tree in McLellan, *Karl Marx: A Biography*, p. 448.
14 Karl Marx, 'On the Jewish Question', in David McLellan (ed.), *Karl Marx: Selected Writings*. Oxford: Oxford University Press, 2000, pp. 46–69.
15 Karl Marx, 'Economic and Philosophical Manuscripts', in David McLellan (ed.), *Karl Marx: Selected Writings*. Oxford: Oxford University Press, 2000, pp. 83–121.
16 Karl Marx, 'Towards a Critique of Hegel's *Philosophy of Right*: Introduction', in David McLellan (ed.), *Karl Marx: Selected Writings*. Oxford: Oxford University Press, 2000, pp. 71–82.
17 Hunt, *Frock-Coated Communist*, pp. 65–6.
18 Karl Marx and Friedrich Engels, 'The Holy Family', in David McLellan (ed.), *Karl Marx: Selected Writings*. Oxford: Oxford University Press, 2000, pp. 145–69.
19 Wheen, *Karl Marx*, (1999), pp. 66–7 and 90–1.
20 Hunt, *Frock-Coated Communist*, p. 128.
21 Gill Hands, *Marx: The Key Ideas*. London: Teach Yourself, Hodder, 2010, p. 193.
22 Karl Marx, 'Preface to A Critique of Political Economy', in David McLellan (ed.), *Karl Marx: Selected Writings*. Oxford: Oxford University Press, 2000, pp. 424–7, p. 426.
23 McLellan, *Karl Marx: A Biography*, pp. 143–57.
24 Terrell Carver, *Marx and Engels: The Intellectual Relationship*. Brighton: Wheatsheaf Books, 1983, pp. 87–94.

Chapter Two

1 Frederick Engels, 'Socialism: Utopian and Scientific', in Karl Marx and Frederick Engels, *Selected Works in One Volume*. London: Lawrence and Wishart, 1968, pp. 375–428, 411; Frederick Engels, 'Engels to J. Bloch in Königsberg', in Karl Marx and Frederick

Engels (eds), *Selected Works in One Volume*. London: Lawrence and Wishart, 1968, pp. 682–3, 682.
2 Engels, 'Socialism: Utopian and Scientific', pp. 411–28.
3 Marx, 'Preface to A Critique of Political Economy', pp. 425–26.
4 Jonathan Wolff, *Why Read Marx Today*. Oxford: Oxford University Press, 2002, pp. 21–8.
5 Peter Osborne (2005), *How to Read Marx*. London: Granta, 2005, p. 84.
6 Karl Marx, 'The Poverty of Philosophy', in David McLellan (ed.), *Karl Marx: Selected Writings*. Oxford: Oxford University Press, 2000, pp. 219–20.
7 Karl Marx, 'Marx to Weydemeyer, 5 March 1852', in David McLellan (ed.), *Karl Marx: Selected Writings*. Oxford: Oxford University Press, 2000, pp. 371–72, 371.
8 Ian Fraser and Lawrence Wilde, *The Marx Dictionary*. London: Continuum, 2011, pp. 47–50.
9 Karl Marx, 'The Class Struggles in France', in David McLellan (ed.), *Karl Marx: Selected Writings*. Oxford: Oxford University Press, 2000, p. 321.
10 Marx, 'Marx to Weydemeyer', p. 372.
11 Stedman Jones, 'Introduction', pp. 67–9.
12 Seed, *Marx: A Guide for the Perplexed*, pp. 36–9.
13 Karl Marx, 'Critique of the Gotha Programme', in Karl Marx and Frederick Engels, *Selected Works in One Volume*. London: Lawrence and Wishart, 1968, pp. 311–31, 322.
14 Marx, 'Marx to Weydemeyer', p. 372; Karl Marx, 'Critique of the Gotha Programme', in David McLellan (ed.), *Karl Marx: Selected Writings*. Oxford: Oxford University Press, 2000, pp. 610–16, 611.
15 Karl Marx and Friedrich Engels, 'The German Ideology', in David McLellan (ed.), *Karl Marx: Selected Writings*. Oxford: Oxford University Press, 2000, pp. 175–208, 184–95.
16 Marx, 'Critique of the Gotha Programme', in McLellan (ed.), *Karl Marx: Selected Writings*, p. 615.

Chapter Three

1 Jon Elster, *An Introduction to Karl Marx*. Cambridge: Cambridge University Press, 1986, p. 105.

2   Karl Marx and Friedrich Engels, *The Communist Manifesto*. New Haven and London: Yale University Press, 2012.

3   The relevant passage from Engels' letter is quoted in Jeffrey C. Isaac (2012), 'Introduction', in Karl Marx and Friedrich Engels, *The Communist Manifesto*. New Haven and London: Yale University Press, 2012, p. 20. A shorter quote from Engels' letter (in a slightly different translation) can be found in Jonathan Sperber, *Karl Marx: A Nineteenth-Century Life*. New York: Liveright Publishing Corporation, 2013, p. 203.

4   Sperber, *Karl Marx*, pp. 156–8 and 196; McLellan, *Karl Marx: A Biography*, p. 157; Wheen, *Karl Marx*, (1999), p. 112.

5   Osborne, *How to Read Marx*, p. 88.

6   For a discussion of Marx's use of metaphors see Terrell Carver, *The Postmodern Marx*. Manchester: Manchester University Press, 1998, pp. 7–23.

7   Stedman Jones, 'Introduction', p. 27.

8   Karl Marx and Friedrich Engels, 'Manifesto of the Communist Party', in Terrell Carver (ed. and trans.), *Marx: Later Political Writings*. Cambridge: Cambridge University Press, 1996, p. 1.

9   Paul Thomas, *Karl Marx*. London: Reaction Books, 2012, p. 97.

10 Carver, *The Postmodern Marx*, p. 13.

11 Karl Marx, 'Theses on Feuerbach', in David McLellan (ed.), *Karl Marx: Selected Writings*. Oxford: Oxford University Press, 2000, p. 173.

12 Karl Marx, *Capital Volume One*. Harmondsworth: Penguin, 1976, p. 102

13 Marx, *Capital Volume One*, p. 103.

14 Fraser and Wilde, *Marx Dictionary*, pp. 66–8 and 78.

15 Fraser and Wilde, *Marx Dictionary*, pp. 66–8 and 78.

16 Lawrence Wilde, 'The Early Development of Marx's Concept of Contradiction' in Mark Cowling and Lawrence Wilde (eds), *Approaches to Marx*. Milton Keynes: Open University Press, 1989, pp. 33–48.

17 Alex Callinicos, *Marxism and Philosophy*. Oxford: Oxford University Press, 1985, p. 56.

18 Marx, 'Preface to A Critique of Political Economy', p. 426.

19 Wolff, *Why Read Marx Today*, pp. 61–4.

20 Marx and Engels, 'Manifesto of the Communist Party', in Carver (ed. and trans.), *Marx*, p. 3.

NOTES

21 Fraser and Wilde, *Marx Dictionary*, p. 194.
22 See Frederic L., Bender's editorial note 4 in Karl Marx, *The Communist Manifesto*. New York and London: WW. Norton and Company, 2013, pp. 62–3.
23 Marx and Engels, 'Manifesto of the Communist Party', in Carver (ed. and trans.), *Marx*, p. 3.
24 Marx and Engels, 'Manifesto of the Communist Party', in Carver (ed. and trans.), *Marx*, p. 10.
25 Marx, 'Preface to A Critique of Political Economy', p. 425.
26 Marx, 'Economic and Philosophical Manuscripts', pp. 85–95.
27 Norman Geras, *Marx and Human Nature: Refutation of a Legend*. London: Verso, 1983, pp. 76–86.
28 Stedman Jones, 'Introduction', pp. 140–4.
29 Karl Marx, 'Wage-Labour and Capital', in David McLellan (ed.), *Karl Marx: Selected Writings*. Oxford: Oxford University Press, 2000, pp. 273–94, 275.
30 Marx, 'Wage-Labour and Capital', p. 275.
31 Marx, 'Wage-Labour and Capital', p. 276.
32 Marx, 'Wage-Labour and Capital', p. 283.
33 Friedrich Engels (2012), 'Principles of Communism', in Karl Marx and Friedrich Engels, *The Communist Manifesto*. New Haven and London: Yale University Press, 2012, p. 20.
34 See Bender's editorial footnote 6 in Karl Marx, *The Communist Manifesto*. New York and London: WW. Norton and Company, 2013, p. 63.
35 Marx and Engels, 'Manifesto of the Communist Party', in Carver (ed. and trans.), *Marx*, p. 3.
36 Sperber, *Karl Marx*, p. 201.
37 Marx, Karl, 'Speech on Free Trade', in David McLellan (ed.), *Karl Marx: Selected Writings*. Oxford: Oxford University Press, 2000, pp. 295–6, 296.
38 Fraser and Wilde, *Marx Dictionary*, p. 92.
39 Marx and Engels, 'Manifesto of the Communist Party', in Carver (ed. and trans.), *Marx*, p. 4.
40 Marx and Engels, 'Manifesto of the Communist Party', in Carver (ed. and trans.), *Marx*, p. 4.
41 Engels, 'Principles of Communism', p. 57.
42 Engels, 'Principles of Communism', p. 57.

43 Marx and Engels, 'Manifesto of the Communist Party', in Carver (ed. and trans.), *Marx*, p. 6.
44 Friedrich Engels, 'Draft of a Communist Confession of Faith', in Karl Marx and Friedrich Engels, *The Communist Manifesto*. New Haven and London: Yale University Press, 2012, p. 47.
45 Engels, 'Principles of Communism', p. 56.
46 Engels, 'Principles of Communism', pp. 57–8.
47 Michael Evans, *Karl Marx*. London: George Allen and Unwin, 1975, p. 37.
48 Seed, *Marx: A Guide for the Perplexed*, pp. 138–42.
49 Michael Levin, 'Marx, Engels and the Parliamentary Path', in Mark Cowling and Lawrence Wilde (eds), *Approaches to Marx*. Milton Keynes: Open University Press, 1989, pp. 149–61.
50 Bhikhu Parekh, *Marx's Theory of Ideology*. London: Croom Helm, 1982, pp. 1–10.
51 Parekh, *Marx's Theory of Ideology*, p. 48.
52 Stedman Jones, 'Introduction', p. 33.
53 Marx and Engels, 'Manifesto of the Communist Party', in Carver (ed. and trans.), *Marx*, p. 11.
54 Jules Townshend, *The Politics of Marxism: The Critical Debates*. London: Leicester University Press, 1996, p. 7.
55 Stedman Jones, 'Introduction', pp. 39–49.
56 Sperber, *Karl Marx*, p. 196.
57 Sperber, *Karl Marx*, p. 199.
58 Marx, 'On the Jewish Question', pp. 59–64.
59 Marx, 'Economic and Philosophical Manuscripts', p. 86.
60 Marx, 'Preface to A Critique of Political Economy', p. 425.
61 Engels, 'Principles of Communism', p. 67.
62 Terry Eagleton, *Marx*. London: Phoenix, 1997, p. 9.
63 Marx, 'Preface to A Critique of Political Economy', p. 426.
64 Parekh, *Marx's Theory of ideology*, pp. 164–85.
65 Marx, 'Preface to A Critique of Political Economy', p. 426.
66 Terry Eagleton, *Why Marx Was Right*. New Haven: Yale University Press, 2011, pp. 190–2.
67 Engels, 'Principles of Communism', p. 67.
68 Engels, 'Principles of Communism', p. 62. The almost identical passage is in Engels, 'Draft of a Communist Confession of Faith', p. 50.

NOTES

69 Sperber, *Karl Marx*, p. 210.
70 Eagleton, *Marx*, p. 45.
71 Geras, *Marx and Human Nature*, pp. 85–6.
72 Thomas, *Karl Marx*, p. 95.
73 Bender, 'Historic and Theoretical Backgrounds', p. 41.
74 David McLellan, 'Introduction', in Karl Marx and Friedrich Engels, *The Communist Manifesto*. Oxford: Oxford University Press, 1998, p. viii.
75 Thomas, *Karl Marx*, pp. 95–7.
76 See Bender's editorial footnote 3 in Karl Marx, *The Communist Manifesto*. New York and London: WW. Norton and Company, 2013, p. 84.
77 Sperber, *Karl Marx*, pp. 310 and 318.
78 Marx, Karl, 'Theories of Surplus Value', in David McLellan (ed.), *Karl Marx: Selected Writings*. Oxford: Oxford University Press, 2000, pp. 429–51, 448.
79 Alex Callinicos, *Marxism and Philosophy*. Oxford: Oxford University Press, 1985, p. 56.
80 Marx, 'Theories of Surplus Value', p. 449.
81 Marx, 'Theories of Surplus Value', p. 449.
82 Marx and Engels, 'Manifesto of the Communist Party', in Carver (ed. and trans.), *Marx*, p. 23.
83 Karl Marx and Frederick Engels, *The German Ideology*. London: Lawrence and Wishart, second edition, 1974, p. 119.
84 Sperber, *Karl Marx*, pp. 181–5.
85 Sperber, *Karl Marx*, p. 171.
86 Marx, and Engels, *The German Ideology*, p. 120.
87 Marx and Engels, 'Manifesto of the Communist Party', in Carver (ed. and trans.), *Marx*, p. 24.
88 See Bender's editorial footnotes 3, 4 and 5 in Karl Marx, *The Communist Manifesto*. New York and London: WW. Norton and Company, 2013, p. 88.
89 Marx and Engels, 'Manifesto of the Communist Party', in Carver (ed. and trans.), *Marx*, p. 24.
90 McLellan, *Karl Marx: A Biography*, pp. 167–8.
91 Paul Thomas, *Karl Marx and the Anarchists*. London: Routledge and Kegan Paul, 1980, pp. 14–17.
92 Thomas, *Karl Marx and the Anarchists*, p. 16.

93   Thomas, *Karl Marx and the Anarchists*, pp. 175–248.
94   Marx and Engels, 'Manifesto of the Communist Party', in Carver (ed. and trans.), *Marx*, p. 26.
95   Engels, 'Principles of Communism', p. 68.
96   Fraser and Wilde, *Marx Dictionary*, pp. 204–5.
97   Bender, 'Historic and Theoretical Backgrounds', pp. 4–5; Edmund Wilson, *To the Finland Station: A Study in the Writing and Acting of History*. London: Fontana, 1960, pp. 73–82.
98   Marx and Engels, 'The German Ideology', p. 198.
99   Marx and Engels, 'The German Ideology', p. 199.
100 Marx and Engels, 'The German Ideology', p. 207.
101 Bender, 'Historic and Theoretical Backgrounds', pp. 5–8; Wilson, *To the Finland Station*, pp. 82–100.
102 Fraser and Wilde, *Marx Dictionary*, pp. 159–61.
103 Robin Blackburn, 'Marxism: Theory of Proletarian Revolution', in Blackburn, Robin (ed.), *Revolution and Class Struggle: A Reader in Marxist Politics*. Glasgow: Fontana/Collins, 1977, pp. 24–68.
104 See Bender's editorial footnote 1 in Karl Marx, *The Communist Manifesto*. New York and London: WW. Norton and Company, 2013, p. 94.
105 Engels, 'Principles of Communism', p. 69.
106 Hunt, *Frock-Coated Communist*, pp. 95–6.
107 McLellan, *Karl Marx: A Biography*, pp. 238–41; Hunt, *Frock-Coated Communist*, pp. 94–6.
108 Engels, 'Principles of Communism', p. 69.
109 See Bender's editorial footnote 8 in Karl Marx, *The Communist Manifesto*. New York and London: WW. Norton and Company, 2013, p. 95.
110 John Cunliffe, 'Marx's Politics – The Tensions in the Communist Manifesto', in Mark Cowling and Lawrence Wilde (eds), *Approaches to Marx*. Milton Keynes: Open University Press, 1989, pp. 102–7.
111 Cunliffe, 'Marx's Politics', p. 106.
112 Engels, 'Principles of Communism', p. 64.
113 Engels, 'Principles of Communism', p. 64.
114 Engels, 'Principles of Communism', p. 64.
115 Seed, *Marx: A Guide for the Perplexed*, pp. 144–7.

116 Marx, 'Class Struggles in France', p. 313.
117 Seed, *Marx: A Guide for the Perplexed*, pp. 129–30; Fraser and Wilde, *Marx Dictionary*, p. 155.
118 Sperber, *Karl Marx*, pp. 357–83.
119 Levin, 'Marx, Engels and the Parliamentary Path'.
120 Hunt, *Frock-Coated Communist*, pp. 339–40.

Chapter Four

1 Hunt, *Frock-Coated Communist*, p. 152.
2 Sperber, *Karl Marx*, pp. 219–36.
3 Stedman Jones, 'Introduction', p. 16.
4 Stedman Jones, 'Introduction', pp. 16–17; Hobsbawm, 'Introduction', pp. 6–7.
5 Marx, Karl, 'The Civil War in France', in David McLellan (ed.), *Karl Marx: Selected Writings*. Oxford: Oxford University Press, 2000, pp. 584–603, 584–96. For commentary, see Sperber, *Karl Marx*, pp. 380–3; McLellan, *Karl Marx: A Biography*, pp. 365–73; Fraser and Wilde, *Marx Dictionary*, pp. 155–6.
6 Hobsbawm, 'Introduction', pp. 8–9.
7 Isaac, 'Introduction', p. 20
8 Stedman Jones, 'Introduction', p. 20.
9 Stedman Jones, 'Introduction', pp. 20–1.
10 Frederick Engels, 'Karl Marx' in Karl Marx and Frederick Engels, *Selected Works in One Volume*. London: Lawrence and Wishart, 1968, pp. 365–74.
11 Brief and very useful discussions of these three works by Lenin can be found in Geoff Boucher, *Understanding Marxism*. Durham: Acumen, 2012, pp. 67–71 and Jonathan Joseph, *Marxism and Social Theory*. Houndmills: Palgrave Macmillan, pp. 38–41.
12 Lenin, V. I. 'The *Communist Manifesto* and the Revolutionary State', in Karl Marx, *The Communist Manifesto*. New York and London: WW. Norton and Company, 2013, p. 127. This extract in Bender's edition of the *Manifesto*, pp. 129–30 is from Lenin's pamphlet 'The State and Revolution'.
13 Fraser and Wilde, *Marx Dictionary*, p. 78.

14 Lenin, 'Communist Manifesto and the Revolutionary State', p. 128.
15 Lenin, 'Communist Manifesto and the Revolutionary State', p. 129.
16 Townshend, *Politics of Marxism*, pp. 94–6.
17 Boucher, *Understanding Marxism*, pp. 75–7.
18 Trotsky, Leon (2013), 'On the Ninetieth Anniversary of the *Communist Manifesto*', in Karl Marx (ed.), *The Communist Manifesto*. New York and London: WW. Norton and Company, 2013, p. 136.
19 Hobsbawm, 'Introduction', pp. 9–10.
20 Karl Marx and Frederick Engels, *Karl Marx: Selected Works in Two Volumes*. London: Lawrence and Wishart, 1942; Karl Marx and Frederick Engels, *Marx/Engels: Selected Works in One Volume*. London: Lawrence and Wishart, 1968.
21 Labour Party, 'Foreword', to Harold J. Laski, *Communist Manifesto: Socialist Landmark*. London: George Allen and Unwin, 1948, p. 6.
22 Joseph, *Marxism and Social Theory*, pp. 28 and 32–4.
23 Bernstein, Eduard (2013), 'Revising the Communist Manifesto', in Karl Marx (ed.), *The Communist Manifesto*. New York and London: WW. Norton and Company, 2013, p. 125. This extract included in Bender's edition of the *Manifesto* is from the Preface to Bernstein's book of 1899 '*Evolutionary Socialism*' (published in some editions under the title '*The Preconditions of Socialism*'). For a brief and clear, albeit critical discussion of Bernstein's theory, see Townshend, *Politics of Marxism*, pp. 20–4.
24 Townshend, *Politics of Marxism*, pp. 30–1.
25 Alex Callinicos, *An Anti-Capitalist Manifesto*. Cambridge: Polity, 2003, p. 20.
26 Callinicos, *Anti-Capitalist Manifesto*, p. 96.
27 Michael Hardt and Antonio Negri, *Empire*. Cambridge, MA and London: Harvard University Press, 2000, p. xii.
28 Hardt and Negri, *Empire*, p. xvi.
29 Hardt and Negri, *Empire*, pp. 63–6.
30 Michael Hardt and Antonio Negri, 'Marx's Mole is Dead!', in Karl Marx, *The Communist Manifesto*. New York and London: WW. Norton and Company, 2013, pp. 209–25. In this article the authors present some of the key points that they made in their book *Empire* and add this new metaphorical element.

NOTES

31 Slavoj Žižek, 'Have Michael Hardt and Antonio Negri Rewritten the *Communist Manifesto* For the Twenty-First Century?', in Karl Marx, *The Communist Manifesto*. New York and London; WW. Norton and Company, 2013, pp. 225–232.

32 Žižek, 'Have Michael Hardt and Antonio Negri Rewritten the *Communist Manifesto*, p. 227.

33 Žižek, 'Have Michael Hardt and Antonio Negri Rewritten the *Communist Manifesto*, p. 228.

34 Townshend, *Politics of Marxism*, p. 262.

35 Townshend, *Politics of Marxism*, p. 272.

INDEX

agriculture 45–6, 80, 87, 90, 119
alienation 9, 10, 11, 33, 37–9, 60, 66, 93
Allende, Salvador 141
American agrarian reformers 108
anarchism 19, 96–8, 155
Anderson, Hans Christian 28
aristocracy 83–7, 107

Babeuf, Gracchus 99–102, 107
Bakunin, Michael 97, 119
Battle in Seattle 142
Bauer, Bruno 8, 10
Bebel, August 134
Bender, Frederic L. 84, 93, 111, 147–50
Bernstein, Eduard 140–1
Blackburn, Robin 106–7, 156
Blanc, Louis 109
Bolsheviks 137
Bonaparte, Louis-Napoleon 148
Bonaparte, Napoleon 6
Bottomore, Tom 156
Boucher, Geoff 155
bourgeoisie 3, 13, 15, 16, 17–18, 20, 30–6, 39–59, 60, 61, 62, 64–72, 74, 76, 82, 83, 85–8, 90, 91, 92, 93–6, 98–9, 99–100, 102, 106, 108, 110, 111–13, 115, 122, 125, 128, 129, 138, 141
  petty 51, 83, 87–90, 92, 95–6, 108, 111

British Labour Party 140
Brussels Democratic Association 40
Burns, Mary 7

Cabet, Étienne, 104, 108
capital 3, 16, 31, 33, 38–40, 48, 49, 52, 57–8, 64, 66–8, 70, 76, 78, 89, 95, 128, 136, 152
capitalism 5, 6, 9, 12, 14, 46–8, 56, 58–9, 60, 72, 73, 78, 82, 84, 111–12, 114, 124, 137, 139, 141–5, 149, 154, 156–7
capitalist mode of production 41, 48, 65, 66, 95, 109, 110, 129–30, 142, 144
capitalist swindle 120
Carew Hunt. R.N. 156
Carlyle, Thomas 85
Carver, Terrell 24, 27, 28, 34, 35, 39, 41, 42, 47, 56, 90, 93, 97, 125, 147–8, 150, 153, 154–5
Chartists, The 107, 108–10
Chinese walls 43–4
Christianity 74, 86
citizenship 65
class struggle 5, 13, 17, 19, 29–30, 50, 54, 57, 73, 82, 96, 97, 99, 102, 104, 106, 114, 122, 128, 138, 156
Cohen, G.A. 155
Collier, Andrew 153

Cologne Communist trial
    (1852) 134
Communist Correspondence
    Committee 12
Communist League 2–4, 12, 17,
    25, 61–2, 73, 81, 100, 106,
    110, 115, 116, 123, 134–5
Corn Law 40
counter-revolutionaries 79–80
Cowling, Mark 154
critical theory 73
critical-utopian communism 83,
    99, 102, 104–6
Cunliffe, John 112–13

Dante 131
democracy 75–6, 78–9, 82, 97,
    114–15, 140, 156
Der Sozialistiche Akademiker 13
Deutsch-Französische Jahbücher 9
dialectic 6–7, 30–1, 34, 41, 42,
    43, 45, 51, 63, 69, 72, 87, 140
Disraeli, Benjamin 85

Eagleton, Terry 73, 75, 81, 154
education 7–8, 15, 53, 71, 78, 137
Egyptian pyramids 42
Elster, Jon 33, 153, 154
emancipation 9, 72, 100, 103,
    111
emigrants 79
Engels, Friedrich
    Communist Manifesto, The ix,
        1–2, 4–5, 7–12, 13–21, 23–6,
        26–9, 29–60, 60–81, 82–107,
        108–25, 126–32, 133–44,
        147–51, 155, 156
    *Condition of the Working Class
        in England, The* 7, 124, 152
    'Draft of a Communist
        Confession of Faith' 7, 12, 49
    German Ideology, The 10–12,
        20, 55, 91–2, 101–2, 152

Holy Family, The 10
'Karl Marx' 136
'Principles of Communism' 7,
    12, 39, 44, 51, 70, 76, 98,
    108, 110
*Socialism: Utopian and
    Scientific* 13
English trade unionists 123, 131
Enlightenment, the 8
Evans, Michael 154
exploitation 16, 18, 35, 39–41,
    43–4, 48, 50, 58–9, 63–7, 71,
    74, 80, 85, 87, 106, 115, 120,
    122

family 8, 10, 41, 70–2, 80, 105
Femia, Joseph V. 156
Feudalism 14, 32–3, 42, 46, 100
feudal mode of production 83,
    94
feudal nobility 34
Feuerbach, Ludwig 7, 29, 60,
    91–2
Fischer, Ernst 155
Fourier, Charles 102–4, 108,
    124
Fourierists 107, 124
Franco-Prussian War 118, 135
Fraser, Ian 154
free development 81, 101–2
free trade 39, 40, 66, 99
French legitimists 85
French Radicals 26, 83, 96, 108,
    110
frightful hobgoblin 28, 29

Geras, Norman 37, 155
German police-spies 26
German Social Democratic
    Party 140
Gothic cathedrals 42
Grimm, Brothers 28
Gruen, Karl 92

INDEX

guilds 32–3, 90
Guizot, François 26

Hands, Gill 11, 153
Hardt, Michael 142–4, 148, 156–7
Hegel, G.W.F. 6–7, 8–9, 31, 55, 91–2
Highgate Cemetery 121
historical materialism 14
Hobsbawm, Eric 149–50
horror story 27, 29, 81
human nature 20, 37, 81, 155
Hunt, Tristram 152

ideology 10–12, 30, 54–5, 60, 73, 91–2, 101–2, 136, 140, 152, 155
immanent critique 73
individualism 9, 65, 81, 104
industrial armies 80
inheritance 79
International Working Men's Association (First International) 123, 125, 126, 131
Isaac, Jeffrey C. 24, 136, 147–8, 150

Johnson, Matthew 155
Jones, Ernest 109
Joseph, Jonathan 156

Laski, Harold 140, 149–50
Lassalle, Ferdinand 19
League of the Just 12, 25, 62
Lenin, V.I. 20, 137–40
Leninism 140
Liebknecht, William 134–5
lumpenproletariat 55

Macdonald, Bradley, J. 156
Macfarlane, Helen 28

McLellan, David ix, 38, 84, 94, 149, 150, 151, 152, 153, 154, 156
manufacturing 51, 80, 87
marriage 70–1, 86
Marx, Heschel/Hienrich 8
Marx, Karl
  Capital: Volume 1 31, 152
  Civil War in France, The 135
  Class Struggles in France 17, 118, 128, 138
  Communist Manifesto, The ix, 1–2, 4–5, 7–12, 13–21, 23–6, 26–9, 29–60, 60–81, 82–107, 108–25, 126–32, 133–44, 147–51, 155, 156
  'Critique of the Gotha Programme' 19, 20, 138
  'Economic and Philosophical Manuscripts' 9, 37, 66
  '1848–9' 17
  German Ideology, The 10–12, 20, 55, 91–2, 101–2, 152
  Holy Family, The 10
  'On the Jewish Question' 8–9, 65
  Poverty of Philosophy, The 16
  Preface to *A Critique of Political Economy* 14, 32, 36, 41, 45, 57, 70, 73, 111, 121, 136
  Theories of Surplus Value 88–9
  'Theses on Feuerbach' 29, 60
  'Towards a Critique of Hegel's Philosophy of Right: Introduction' 9
  Wage-Labour and Capital 38–9, 49
Marx–Engels–Lenin Institute (Moscow) 139
Marxism 4, 73, 97, 137, 139, 140, 141, 145, 147, 154, 155–6
Marxism-Leninism 137

INDEX

Marxists Internet Archive 151, 155
materialist conception of
  history 10, 11–12, 13–15, 29, 70, 72–3, 83, 86, 87, 93, 94, 100, 105, 111, 120, 122, 124, 129–30, 136
Matthews, Betty 156
medieval burgesses 87
Mensheviks 137
Metternich, Klemens von 26
modernity 16, 18, 19, 85
monarchy 34, 84–5, 111
Moore, Samuel viii, 1, 24, 27, 35, 56, 57, 93, 124, 148, 151

nationality 71–2
Negri, Antonio 142–4, 148, 156–7
Neue Rheinische Zeitung 38
nursery tale 27, 29

obshchina 120
Opium War 44
Osborne, Peter 16, 26, 153
Owen, Robert 102–4, 108, 124
Owenites 107, 124

Parekh, Bhikhu 155
Paris Commune 118, 135
Parisian communards 135
Paris Workers' Congress (1889) 125
peasantry 3, 50, 64, 87–8, 90, 111, 120, 127, 148
Polish Democratic Society 111
productive forces 11, 14–15, 16, 19, 20, 32, 36, 41, 45–9, 59, 69, 70, 73–4, 76, 82, 88–90, 95, 97, 101–2, 105, 109, 111–14, 117–18, 120, 129–30
professional revolutionaries 137
proletariat 7, 9, 10, 13, 14, 15, 17–18, 19, 20, 29–30, 33, 35, 40, 46, 49–59, 60–3, 65, 71–3, 75–7, 80, 82, 84, 86, 87–8, 90, 92, 94–5, 97–103, 105–6, 109, 111–15, 116, 118, 119–21, 122, 123, 125–6, 128, 130–1, 134, 137–9, 141, 142–4, 148
  dictatorship of 20, 138
Proudhon, Pierre-Joseph 78–9, 96–8, 107

Radical Party (Swiss) 110
Red Republican, The 134
reductio ad absurdum 27, 29
Reform Act (1832) 85
Réformistes, The 107, 108–9
religion 6, 8–9, 11, 56, 74, 86
revolution 1–2, 3–4, 4–5, 10, 11, 13, 14, 15, 16, 17–18, 19, 20, 25, 30, 33–4, 36, 38, 40, 42, 46, 48, 52, 53, 54, 55, 56–9, 60, 62, 63, 64, 65, 70, 72, 73, 74, 75–80, 81, 82, 84, 86, 91, 92, 94, 95, 97–8, 99–100, 101, 102, 103–4, 105, 106–7, 109, 110, 111–15, 116, 117, 118, 119, 121, 122, 123, 125, 127–8, 129–31, 132, 133, 134, 135, 136, 137–8, 139, 140, 141, 144, 148, 153, 154, 156
  dual 3, 33
  French (1789) 3, 4, 5, 63, 65, 81, 82, 125
  French (1830) 84, 125
  French (February) (1848) 118, 125, 129
  German (1848) 4
Rheinische Zeitung 8
rights 9, 64–5, 77, 79, 82
Roman aqueducts 42

Saint-Simon, Henri de 102–4, 108
Schapper, Karl 25

INDEX

Seed, John 153
Shaftsbury, Lord 85
Singer, Peter 153
Sismondi, Charles, Simonde de 88–9, 107
Social-Democrats (French) 109–10
socialism 4–5, 10, 13, 18–19, 20, 81, 82–108, 123, 124, 131, 137, 139, 140
  Christian 86–7
  clerical 86
  conservative or bourgeois 83, 96–9, 107
  critical-utopian 30, 61, 83, 90, 99, 102–6, 108, 124
  feudal 83–6
  petty-bourgeois 83, 87–90
  reactionary 83–96
  true 83, 91–6, 107
spectre 26–9, 81, 83
Sperber, Jonathan 152
Stalin, Josef 20, 139–40
Stedman Jones, Gareth 134, 136, 148, 150
Stirner, Max 38, 97, 101

tax 45, 78
Taylor, A.J.P. 149–50

Ten Hours Act 53, 76, 125
theory of value 37
Thomas, Paul 28, 82, 84, 152–3, 155
Townshend, Jules 59, 145, 156
trades unions 52, 123
Trotsky, Leon 139–40

vanguard of the proletariat 137
von Westphalen, Jenny 8
Vorwärts! 10

wage labour 38–9, 41, 48–9, 51, 64, 65–6, 68, 89
Weydemeyer, Joseph 17–18, 138
Wheen, Francis 152
Wilde, Lawrence 154
Wilson, Edmund 156
Wolfe, Bertram D. 156
Wolff, Jonathan 15, 154
World Economic Forum 142
World Social Forum 142
World Trade Organization 141
Wright Mills, C. 156

Young England movement 85
Young Hegelians 6–8, 92

Žižek, Slavoj 143–4